AF601656

READING EARLY HANDWRITING 1500 – 1700

Mark Forrest

Reading Early Handwriting
1500 – 1700

Published by the British Association for Local History 2019
Chester House, 68 Chestergate
Macclesfield SK11 6DY
01625 664524
admin@balh.org.uk

© British Association for Local History 2019
www.balh.org.uk
All rights reserved

Typeset in ITC New Baskerville by John Chandler

ISBN 978-0-948140-04-4

The front cover illustration is an extract from Ralph Treswell's survey of Lord Chancellor Hatton's property in Kettering, Northants, 1585, NRO LM/272 (reproduced by kind permission of Northamptonshire Record Office).

The back cover illustration shows a trompe l'oeil painting by Thomas Warrener of Edinburgh, who was working between about 1673 and 1713. It is full of hidden messages and political imagery, celebrating the 'information revolution' of the late seventeenth century, as printing of tracts and broadsheets contributed to a more politically informed popular culture. It is very closely modelled on Simon van Hoostraten's 1663 painting 'A Pamphlet History of the Rump Parliament' which uses the same devices – quill, manuscript tract, seals and other objects. The parchment documents and wax seals attached by tape or ribbon are immediately recognisable to anyone who has used deed bundles in an archive, but quills are less familiar: the feathers of that on the right are trimmed and shaped in the standard way – despite the popular image, people did not write with long feathers but with short ones, about the same size as a fountain pen (reproduced by kind permission of the National Gallery of Scotland).

Contents

Preface

Working with original sources is fundamental to the practice of history. To be faced with the words actually written by the subject and contemporaries of our research is a thrilling – and humbling – experience. But our initial enthusiasm in tracking down an important document can rapidly be quenched if we cannot read it. As historians we have a duty to learn how to decipher unfamiliar styles of handwriting, and a responsibility to record accurately the words communicated to us by people long dead. Like any skill it comes with practice, of course, but it also helps if you have a guide, and perhaps a similar document transcribed for you, so can see what it is likely to say.

The first edition of *Reading Tudor and Stuart Handwriting*, as it was then entitled, was prepared by the late Lionel Munby for the British Association for Local History in 1988, and a second extended edition, fully revised by Steve Hobbs and Alan Crosby, was published in 2002. It has proved invaluable to very many historians over the years, but the stock is now exhausted, and we approached Mark Forrest, of Dorset History Centre and formerly the National Archives, to undertake a thorough revision – in reality to produce a new book. This he has done, with the consent and encouragement of the previous revisers. We are extremely grateful to him.

The result is not only a concise and practical palaeographical guide to the hands in use during the sixteenth and seventeenth centuries – which any historian venturing before 1700 will encounter and may be baffled by – but it is also a compendium of information about all the other potential snags facing users of documents from this period. So there are helpful explanations of dates, numbers, names and measurements, and a discussion of the various conventions for transcription. All this is followed by over twenty facsimiles of documents, accompanied by transcriptions and a brief commentary, thus enabling users to develop their palaeographical skills, and to relate common classes of documents they might encounter to these worked examples.

This book exists not only through Mark's efforts, but thanks also to the kindly co-operation of Steve Hobbs, Alan Crosby and Philip Judge, some of whose work has been incorporated from the second edition. It also benefits from the suggestions and oversight of officers and committee members of BALH. Particular thanks go to Daniel Williams, Northamptonshire Record Office; Isabel Sullivan, Surrey History Centre; Katherine Kinrade, Oxfordshire History Centre; Judith Yeo, Suffolk Record Office; Paul Dryburgh, the National Archives; Donna Marshall, Wiltshire & Swindon History Centre; and to all the other archivists, archives offices and owners who have permitted us to reproduce extracts from documents in their ownership and care.

John Chandler
Chair, BALH Publishing Committee

Introduction

Tudor and Stuart documents have never been so accessible for research of all kinds. Academic and genealogical websites are increasing their content of images of original records and the researcher, armed with a digital camera, is able to take hundreds of photographs during a single visit to an archive. Whereas studying original material was once largely the preserve of the postgraduate or academic it is now commonplace for local and family historians to visit their local record office to find new sources of information. Developments in history teaching at secondary level have encouraged study based on the critical analysis of sources, and local history has become integrated into the school curriculum. More Tudor and Stuart documents are being read in the twenty-first century than at any time since the seventeenth century.

Acquiring the tools for the job goes a lot further than a digital camera or a pencil and notepad. Reading the documents is a skill that takes time to develop alongside an understanding of the context in which they were created. Reading old handwriting, or palaeography, is an art that allows the researcher to obtain a unique view of the past by studying documents that may not have been seen for hundreds of years. Transcribing accurately makes them available for others and this is where the most care is required; potentially once an error is committed to print or published online it may easily be repeated by those who do not have access to the original source.

This book is for the local or family historian, student or researcher beginning to work with English documents written between around 1500 and 1700. It examines the two principal writing styles – Secretary and Italic – as well as the more traditional Court hands which continued to develop in parallel with them. The same hands were used for writing Latin documents, as during this period (and until 1733) Latin remained a formal legal language. For those without a knowledge of Latin an idea of the content and variety of legal documents can be obtained from those produced during the Commonwealth when, between 1651 and 1659, English was used for all purposes.

There are certain 'tricks' or methods that are helpful when starting to read and transcribe documents. Foremost of these is to actually read every letter: don't guess. Most English speakers will read a printed text without examining every letter, but when looking at a historic manuscript this is essential as it is all too easy to see what the reader *thinks* is written, rather than what is *actually* written. When starting on a new text the following processes may help the task from becoming too daunting:

- Read a large section, or the whole text, through before starting to transcribe. This will give a lot of known words and letter combinations as well as assisting with those that prove difficult on first reading.
- Look for similar examples of the same letter form elsewhere in the text.
- Cover over part of a word, often the initial letter, to see if the rest can be read.
- Copy the script to see how the writer has formed each letter and how one letter leads into another.

- Only look at the context of a word once the majority of a text has been transcribed, otherwise an incorrect assumption might influence the interpretation of the remainder of the document.
- If a word is identified by the context go back and trace each letter to make sure that the correct identification has been made.

As late as the nineteenth century spelling was not standardised, even by writers within the same text; many local dialect terms were in use; and certain words have become obsolete or changed their meanings. Phonetic spelling was widespread and there was no concept of a 'wrong' spelling. So if a word looks improbable, but there is no doubt about its transcription, a phonetic reading may reveal its meaning. When identifying fragments in the E179 tax class at the National Archives editors found a document headed 'Dodeleye'. With a West Midlands accent it seemed possible that it referred to Dudley, and this was confirmed by comparison with similar documents.

In the following section model alphabets are reproduced as a guide. They identify the ideal, or most common, letter forms which can be found in English documents from the sixteenth and seventeenth centuries. The first is a Secretary hand, which is encountered in almost every kind of document and would be expected for parish records, wills, borough records, manorial records and local courts. The second is Court hands, which were used by trained lawyers and their clerks and were the hands expected in the central courts at Westminster. Secretary hand and Court hands were different scripts, but they borrowed from each other as well as from Italic, and they developed over the two hundred years covered by this guide.

Tudor and Stuart England was more literate than might be supposed. Gentlemen and merchants exchanged letters, people of all classes read the bible, clerks kept the accounts of courts, manors and boroughs, and pamphlets were disseminated from printing presses. Literacy did not imply that an individual could both read and write with equal proficiency, since the ability to read was significantly more common. It is always worth remembering that almost all texts were written to be read by someone else, no matter how obscure they seem to a modern reader.

The hands

In the sixteenth and seventeenth centuries people were taught to write in several different styles and these years saw more variation than previous centuries. As printing developed and spread it was influenced by, and itself influenced, manuscript styles or 'hands'. The style that a writer learned depended upon their location, occupation and what was in fashion. Once acquired it would be retained throughout the writer's lifetime and, particularly in remote areas, archaic elements might be passed to the next generation. Three hands predominated in these centuries: medieval Book hand, Secretary and Italic, supplemented by the mannered Court hands which were taught to scribes in the London-based law courts.

Medieval Book hands originated in ninth-century scripts developed for the court of Charlemagne when it was found that the Holy Roman Empire was impossible to administer without a common, mutually intelligible, script. Looking for a classical model for this hand the Frankish clerks viewed Roman inscriptions as a definitive model and the letters were derived from these carved letter forms. Immediately this presented a problem for scribes using quills, ink and parchment. Letters designed

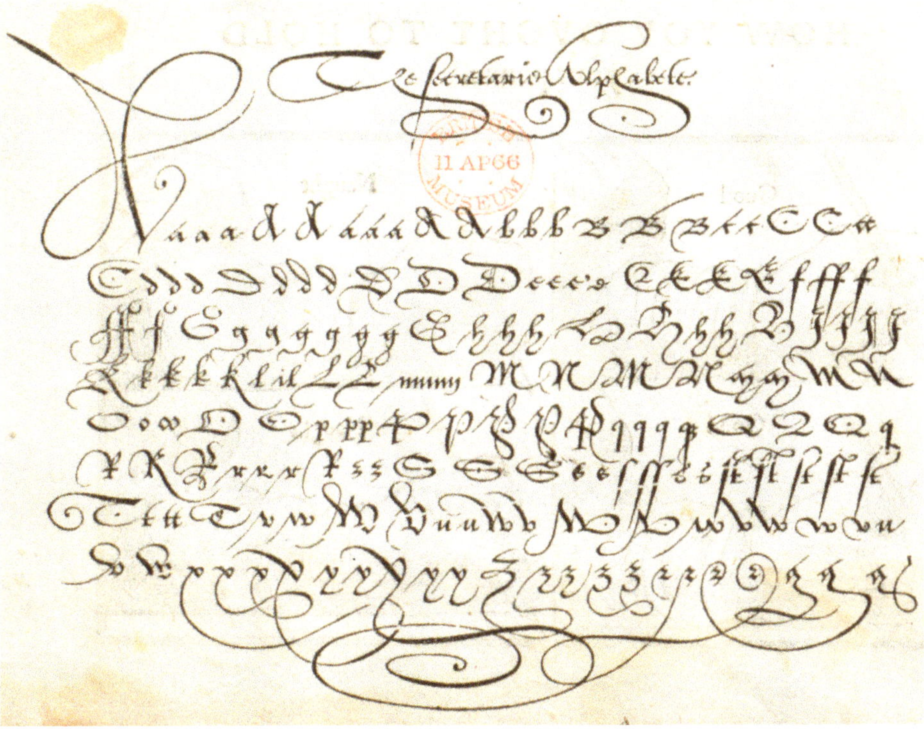

The Secretary Alphabet, printed by John de Beauchesne and John Baildon in A Booke containing divers sortes of hands , as well the English as French secretarie with the Italian, Roman, chancery & court hands. *First published 1570.*

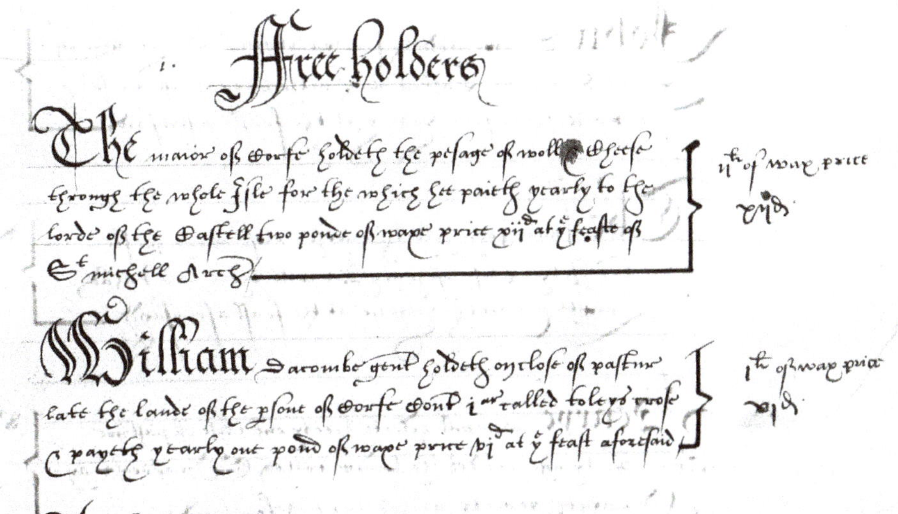

1. Free holders

The maior of Corfe holdeth the pesage of woll & chese through the whole Isle for the which hee paith yearly to the lorde of the Castell two pounde of waxe price xvjd at ye feaste of St Michell Arch — ijli of wax price xvjd

William Dacombe gent holdeth one close of pasture latt the lande of the parson of Corfe cont' i acr called [illegible] & payeth yearly one pond of waxe price vjd at ye feast aforesaid — jli of wax price vjd

Secretary Hand as written by a professional: a section from Ralph Treswell's Survey of Purbeck, *compiled 1585-1586, Dorset History Centre, D-BKL/E/A/1*

A general Alphabet of the Old Law Hands.

An alphabet of Court hands demonstrating many letter forms from Andrew Wright A Court Hand Restored, *first published in 1776*

to be carved were not ideal for joined up, or cursive, writing and so the manuscript forms gradually developed to accommodate the needs of the clerks, and the late medieval book hands were heavily abbreviated and had letters that ran together. These hands were in common use only for the first couple of decades of the sixteenth century, but their abbreviations and some of the more complex capital letters persisted and were adopted into Secretary and Italic hands.

Secretary hand was the dominant form of handwriting used in England in the sixteenth century. It is unfamiliar to the modern reader and, although it is similar to the Gothic character set, commonly used for printed works in Germany until the mid-twentieth century, it is the furthest from modern typesets. Many of the letter forms are easy to recognise when presented as an alphabet, but become more difficult when written together in a text with unfamiliar spellings, abbreviations and letters from one line interfering with those above and below.

Italic handwriting developed in Italy in the early sixteenth century and became common in England in the seventeenth century. *It is similar to a modern italic typeface,* characteristically leaning to the right. Study guides for children and scholars, such as the *Booke containing divers sortes of hands* produced by the Huguenot exile Jean de Beauchesne and John Baildon in London in 1570, contained sample alphabets of the different hands and presented them in short texts.

Both Secretary and Italic hands retained some medieval abbreviations and unfamiliar letter forms. Naturally, when students were taught to write in two styles over several centuries, they would blend characteristics of both together as 'bastard' hands which are often notable for Secretary letter forms and the Italic slant to the right.

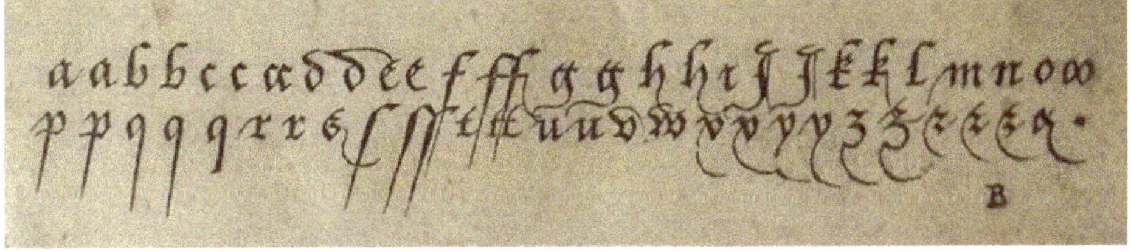

The Court hands used in the London courts such as Chancery and the Court of Common Pleas and in some ecclesiastical courts were taught to the scribes who worked there as part of their training. They were occasionally used for wills and other legal documents. These are heavily stylised scripts based upon medieval Book hand. To add to the complexity the scribes in these courts had 'set' hands for legal documents and 'fast' hands for administrative records.

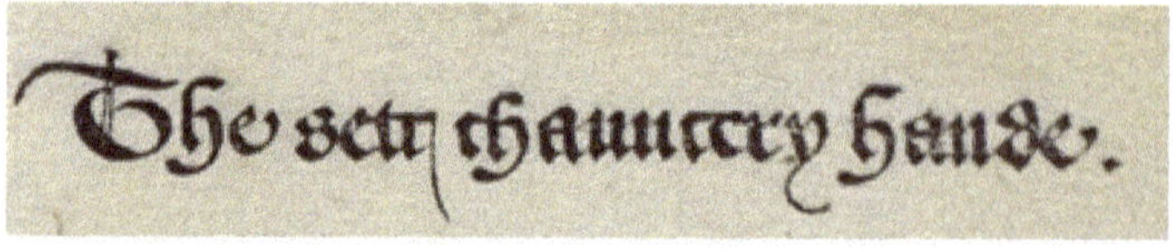

Most of the examples in this book are of Secretary hands. A further alphabet compiled from the parish registers of Gillingham, Dorset, illustrates how these Secretary alphabets might appear in context: all of these letters are from a single year of the parish register, 1648. The letter forms are similar to those outlined by Beauchesne and Baildon two generations earlier, but some features have become exaggerated, some by the individual scribe and others as a general shift in the fashion of how a particular letter was presented.

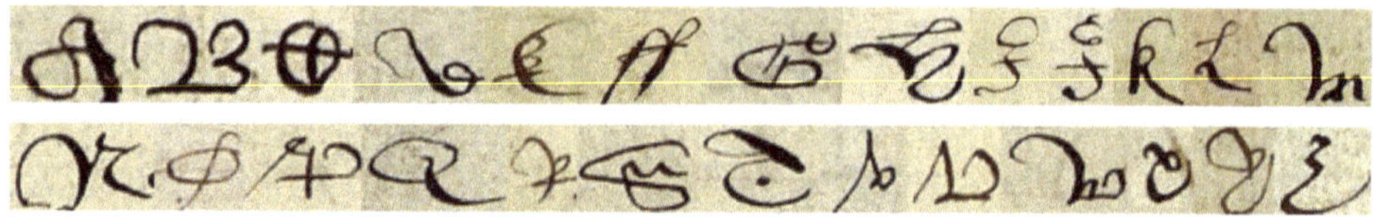

Secretary and Bastard Secretary hands were the most common throughout the majority of the sixteenth and seventeenth centuries, used by all scribes from court clerks to local administrators and private correspondents. Examples of the other hands have been provided to emphasise their differences and those features that are likely to present most difficulty to the modern reader.

The Secretary alphabet

Sixteenth and seventeenth century letter forms are sometimes unfamiliar to the modern reader. Some seem needlessly complicated and derive from medieval forms, others more closely resemble different modern letters. However, as scribes were taught to write in a particular style, once the reader knows the handwriting of one scribe it is much easier to read the hands of their contemporaries.

It is more difficult to write with a quill pen on parchment or handmade paper than with a pencil or ballpoint pen on mass produced paper. Identifying individual letters, working out how they were formed and how they join to the adjacent letters, reveals how the scribe produced words by taking the easiest method to create the letter forms with the available equipment. When encountering a new hand or confronted with a difficult passage it is often helpful to copy the text mimicking the letter forms to establish how the scribe formed each letter and how they joined to each other.

Aa Capital **A** is similar to the modern form, but the initial ascender is usually curved and the cross line come up from the base of the first ascender. Like several other letters capital **A** may have two forms, the other being an enlarged version of lower case **a**. Small **a** has two usual forms: a modern printed **a** or in two sections resembling **oi** without the dot.

Bb Capital **B** may be more complicated than the reader expects. An initial ascender is often a distance from the two curved sections of the descender. Occasionally a medieval capital form persists as a circular letter divided in the centre by vertical and horizontal lines and a tail ascending to the right from the top. Small **b** resembles a modern **b**, but often with a looped ascender.

Cc Capital **C** is commonly called 'hot cross bun' **C**, a circular letter with crossing internal vertical and horizontal lines. In letter versions the right side may be open and the horizontal line omitted. Small **c** is one of the more difficult letters to recognise. It may resemble a modern **c**, or have the lower cross stroke omitted to resemble a modern **r**, or omit the lower horizontal stroke and drop the upper horizontal to resemble a small **t**.

Dd Capital **D** is sometimes resembles the modern form, but may also be another circular letter, sometimes open at the left side, and with a vertical down stroke in the centre. Small **d** resembles the modern form but the ascender may both lean to the left and be looped.

Ee Capital **E** is circular or open to the right with a vertical downstroke to the centre and a **z** in the middle. Small **e** may take several forms, often in the same manuscript. Most frequently it is a mirror of a modern **e**, or resembles a modern **c** formed by one stroke to make the back and bottom horizontal and a second stroke to make the top horizontal.

Ff Capital **F** is usually formed by placing two small **f**'s together. Small **f** is similar to the modern form, although the cross stroke is often faint.

Gg Capital **G** is a rounded letter, usually open at the top right and bisected by a vertical stroke. Small **g** may take the form of a modern written **g** with the tail open or as a typescript with the tail closed to form an 8.

Hh Capital **H** closely resembles a modern small h without the top half of the second ascender. It may be a long letter with the initial ascender some distance from the shoulder. Small h is a particular characteristic of Secretary hands, often called 'shoulderless' **h** the final stroke drops below the line.

The letters **I** and **J** are interchangeable and have one written form. The capitals more closely resemble **J**, sometimes with a second parallel ascender or a central cross stroke. The small letter is a single down stroke, like a modern **i**, but sometimes without a dot.

Kk Capital **K** and small **k** are formed in the same way as the modern letters, but with the upper right strokes looped back to join the ascender. A common variant for both forms is 'kicking' **k** in which the lower right stroke is raised from the line as if it is kicking the following letter.

Ll Capital **L**'s ascender may be doubled, looped or rising from the centre of the base stroke rather than the left. Small **l** is like the modern form or may be looped.

Mm Capital **M** has two common forms: one similar to the modern form with a curved tail from the final ascender beneath the letter, the other split almost in two resembling a modern **L** before an oversized **n**. Small **m** is a series of three down strokes termed minims as in medieval hands the word minim consisted of ten identical down strokes.

Nn Capital **N** is similar to a modern small **n**, but variously with tails at the top and bottom for the ascenders, and a dot or vertical line in the centre. Small **n** consists of two minims.

Oo Capital **O** is circular with a central vertical line; unlike other rounded letters it is always enclosed. Small **o** resembles the modern **o**, but may be more square than circle.

Pp Capital **P** is one of the more difficult letters. The tail may drop below the line and carry one of a number of abbreviation strokes. It may be open at the top, like a **U** with a tail. Small **p** is like the modern letter, but may also be open at the top.

Qq Capital **Q** is rarely found in English documents except in the word Queen, it may take the form of a modern capital with the tail extending to the right along the line, or as a large version of small **q** whose tail curls to the left.

Rr Capital **R** is much like the modern form with a tail from the top of the ascender and the right leg lifting to kick the following letter. Small **r** has more forms than any other letter; one looks like modern **r**, another like **z** and a third, 'flat bottomed r', has a vertical stroke and a horizontal stroke preceding a modern typescript **r**, occasionally a 'long **r**' may drop below the line.

Ss Capital **S** is like the modern form with the lower part enclosed so the whole letter becomes more circular. Small **s** has many forms: 'long **s**' dropping below the line, 'terminal **s**' is found at the end of a word and is a circle with a tail, like a 6, extending from the top to the right, or looks like a modern e with the bottom stroke extending below the line,'toppling s' is an enclosed version of the typescript form, almost an 8, but leaning to the right.

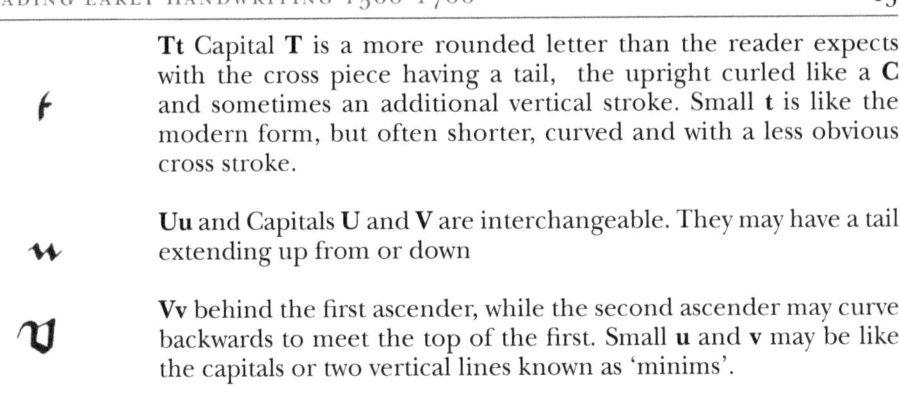

Tt Capital **T** is a more rounded letter than the reader expects with the cross piece having a tail, the upright curled like a **C** and sometimes an additional vertical stroke. Small **t** is like the modern form, but often shorter, curved and with a less obvious cross stroke.

Uu and Capitals **U** and **V** are interchangeable. They may have a tail extending up from or down

Vv behind the first ascender, while the second ascender may curve backwards to meet the top of the first. Small **u** and **v** may be like the capitals or two vertical lines known as 'minims'.

Ww Capital **W** is probably the most complicated capital. It has an initial ascender which may be curved, have a tail, or a horizontal foot like an **L**, this is followed by a capital **U** which may have the final ascender curved back on itself or divided into two loops. Small **w** is like the modern form with the final stroke curving back at the top, or as a series of three down strokes.

Xx Capital **X** has the lower left leg dropping below the line and the two right strokes formed as a single loop. Small **x** is the same as the capital, both are easy to spot as Roman numerals, but may be confused with '&' in a text.

Yy Capital **Y** and small **y** are like the modern forms, but both have tails that drop below the line and curve away to the right.

Zz Capital **Z** and small **z** are much like their modern forms, but both may drop below the line.

Letters fall into groups. It is worth noting those letters that are frequently mistaken for each other or contain common characteristics.

- Circular capitals: C, D, E, G, O, Q.
- Split capitals: B, M, W.
- Letters that closely resemble each other; s and f, K and R.

The letters i, m, n and u are all written as a series of down strokes without separation between the letters. These down strokes are known as minims and the word minimum might look like |||||||||||||||. By knowing the context and counting the minims it is usually possible to work out the letters.

The language

During the period 1500-1700 English, and occasionally Welsh, gradually replaced Latin in most documents. However, most legal documents were written in Latin for the whole period and continued to be so until 1733 with the brief exception of the Commonwealth, 1650-1660, when English was used for all court proceedings including those that took place in Wales.

In non-statutory documents the transition from Latin took place in different locations at different times, with London and East Anglia generally being the earliest to change, and certain types of document were usually written in English before others. For instance private correspondence and wills were often in English by 1500, with taxation and customs records by 1550 and parish registers by 1600. Manorial documents varied depending upon their legal content and the preference of the scribe, with the court proceedings almost all in Latin, but surveys, rentals and presentments in English. Welsh was used in family papers and local estate administration, but very rarely for official records and never for court proceedings.

Latin headings might be used as standard in documents principally written in English to provide legal validation, for instance for bonds or apprenticeship indentures, while English wills were usually proved in Latin. For the researcher without Latin most of the sense of these documents can be obtained from the English sections, but this often leaves a nagging doubt as to whether everything has been wrung out of the text and several starter guides listed in the bibliography offer help in the interpretation of the most common Latin documents.

The tools: paper, parchment, ink and quills

By the start of the sixteenth century imported paper was already in use and it was being produced in England by 1600, but parchment was retained by some scribes, particularly for legal documents, into the twentieth century and at the turn of the millennium there was still one commercial parchment manufacturer in England.

Parchment can be made from any animal hide, but was most commonly sheep, goat or calf skin. The term vellum generally refers to fine calf skin. Parchment is more robust than paper and as long as it is kept away from water and pests it will last for centuries. Paper, however, produced in large quantities for the new printing industry, was cheaper, lighter and easier to bind into volumes.

Ink was often made by the scribe. Iron sulphate, gum-arabic, vinegar and oak galls (the growths created when the gall wasp lays its eggs on the underside of an oak leaf) were combined in various quantities. If it was too acidic or contained too much iron the ink would rot or rust through the paper, if there was not enough gum-arabic it would not stick to the surface of the parchment, but these problems are rare and remarkably few documents show signs of deterioration due to poor quality materials. Unfortunately, the conditions in which they were kept have often proved to be more hazardous.

Quills were cut and re-cut by the scribe as they wrote. Goose feathers were most common, but those of any large bird might be used. Writing with a quill is different from writing with a fountain pen; the ink is more likely to pool and blot and this was more likely when the quill was removed from the writing surface. A cursive, flowing, hand in which the scribe moved at a regular speed was encouraged by the writing materials.

Numbers

The only characters to express numbers in use in England until the fourteenth century were Roman numerals. Arabic numbers gradually became popular during the fifteenth century and began to dominate after the introduction of printing in the mid-sixteenth century, when it was much easier for a printer to construct a number from Arabic than Roman numerals. But Roman numerals remained popular in written records throughout the sixteenth and seventeenth centuries, sometimes interspersed with Arabic, so in the same text a date might be given in Roman numerals and currency in Arabic or vice versa.

The core Roman numbers are: i for 1, V for 5, X for 10, L for 50, C for 100, D for 500 and M for 1000. All other numbers are created by the order of the core numbers. A smaller number preceding a larger number is subtracted: ix is 9, whereas a smaller number following a larger number is added: vj is 6.

Note that when writing Roman numerals the 'i' at the end of a sequence of numbers is usually represented as a 'j': thus ij is 2, iij is 3, viij is 8. This useful device prevented forgery and meant that the amount could not be altered – particularly in financial documents. The form of the number *4* was usually *iiij* in the sixteenth century and commonly *iv* by the late seventeenth, similarly *14*, *xiiij* and *xiv*. This gradual change took place in the south of England earlier than in the north and is another change brought about by printers who never had enough 'i's in their character sets!

Roman Numerals

1	i	19	xix	100	C
2	ij	20	XX	200	CC
3	iij	21	XXj	300	CCC
4	iv *or* iiij	22	XXij	400	CD
5	V	23	XXiij	500	D
6	vj	24	XXiv *or* XXiiij	600	DC
7	vij	25	XXV	700	DCC
8	viij	26	XXvj	800	DCCC
9	ix	27	XXvij	900	CM
10	X	28	XXviij	1000	M
11	xj	29	XXix		
12	xij	30	XXX	*Some example numbers:*	
13	xiij	40	XL		
14	xiv *or* xiiij	50	L	197	CXCvij
15	XV	60	LX	2254	MMCCLiv or mmccliv
16	xvj	70	LXX	63	LXiij
17	xvij	80	LXXX	289	CCLXXXix
18	xviij	90	XC	648	DCXLviij or dcxlviij

There is some variation in how a scribe may choose to represent larger and more complicated numbers that require addition and subtraction of characters. For instance 1949 might be written as MCMIL, or MDCCCCXXXXIX.

Superscript numbers are used to indicate multiples, usually multiples of 20 (known as a *score*): iiij^{xx} represents 4 times 20 making 80, while vi^{xx} represents 6 times 20 making 120.

Currency and measurements

Several works provide detailed descriptions of currencies and measurements in use during the Tudor and Stuart periods. The introduction here is a guide to which should be added many local variations.

The basic unit of currency was the pound sterling, denoted by the symbol £, a stylised form of the capital 'L' of the Latin *libra.* Within the pound were 20 shillings, abbreviated to s. for *solidus*; and each shilling contained 12 pennies, abbreviated to d. for *denarius.* A half penny was abbreviated to ob. for *obolus*; and a quarter penny or *farthing* to q. for *quarteria.* Instead of the pound sums were sometimes expressed as multiples of a *mark*, 13s. 4d.; or half a *mark*, 6s. 8d. also known as a *noble.*

A sum of money might be expressed in a text as £1 3s. 4d., frequently with the abbreviated letter superscript as £1 3^{s} 4^{d}, or in a list of accounts as 01:03:04. Commonly a larger sum might be expressed using smaller units, in the previous example as 23s. 4d. or 17d. instead of 1s. 5d.

Measurements for weight are more complex. The standard pound weight is the most common and usually abbreviated as *lb*, plural *lbs*, also a contraction of *libra*; it is divided into 16 ounces, abbreviated to oz. But there are numerous other weights for particular products: grains in bushels (*bsh*) and quarters (*qtr*), tar in barrels, and wine and oil in tuns. For products of different weights the same term was sometimes used: a clove of butter or cheese might be 7 or 8 pounds in different regions, but was always 7 pounds when applied to wool; butter and cheese always had two cloves to the stone, but might have 16 or 21 stones to the wey, while a wey of wool contained 13 stones.

Measurements of length were more standard: 1 foot contained 12 inches, 1 yard contained three feet, 1 rod, pole or perch contained 5½ yards, 1 furlong contained 40 rods and 1 mile contained 8 furlongs. The only other commonly used measurement was the chain of 66 feet (it is still recognised as the length of a cricket wicket). If standard units of length had always been applied then units of area should also be standard: the square inch and square yard leading to a square rod, pole or perch of 30.25 square yards, a rood or 40 square rods and an acre of 4 roods. But this system had to be superimposed upon some very ancient local customary measurements.

The rod might consist of only 5 yards in Hampshire, but might be as many as 8½ in Lancashire. Within Cumberland the rod might be of 6, 6⅔, 7 or 7⅑ yards and in consequence the Cumbrian customary acre might be one fifth or two thirds larger than the standard acre. Local husbandmen knew the size of their holdings in customary acres and did not wish to see them 'reduced' by land surveyors, so the customary acre persisted well beyond the start of the eighteenth century.

Other local terms muddy the waters: ferlings, goads and parrocks were all small areas, less than one acre, sometimes equivalent to a rod. Yardlands or virgates and bovates or oxgangs were based upon the amount of land necessary to support an extended family so they varied from one place to another depending upon the quality of the land; in Surrey the virgate might be as small as 5 acres at Wimbledon, while it was 15 at Cobham, 20 at Pyrford, 21 at Cheam and 32 at Farleigh. It is always best to be aware that even when a measurement looks as if it is a standard term it may have a local use, and where possible should be checked against later records.

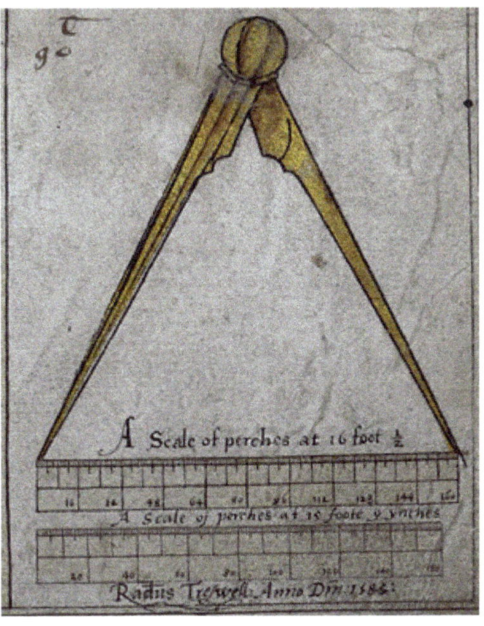

In 1585 Ralph Treswell helpfully produced his maps of Purbeck with two scales, one for the standard perch of 16½ feet and one for the local customary perch of 15¾ feet.

Dates

Early modern dating can be extremely confusing. An excellent introduction is L. Munby's *Dates and Time: a handbook for local historians* and access to a copy of C. R. Cheney's *Handbook of Dates for students of British history* is strongly recommended for any date that needs to be converted from one system to another. A few basic points are worth stating here to avoid the most obvious pitfalls.

Dating of years followed two styles, and it is important to recognise that the habit of dating documents was by no means universal during the early modern period. The more familiar style *Anno Domini*, or 'in the year of our Lord' also known as the 'year of Grace' is the style used today. Much more frequent in the early sixteenth century was the 'regnal year', the year of the reign of the current sovereign. Thus a document might be dated 'the fifth of July in the seventh year of the reign of our sovereign lord Charles by the grace of God King of England, Scotland, France and Ireland'. This would be Charles I as without the benefit of foresight the scribe would not have anticipated there being a Charles II. The 5th of July in the 7th year of his reign fell in 1631 as his regnal years dated from his accession on 27 March 1625, so the date in the document is 5 July 1631. Gradually the 'year of our Lord' replaced the 'regnal year' and during the sixteenth and seventeenth centuries many scribes gave both versions.

The use of regnal years presents a couple of minor problems in the sixteenth and seventeenth centuries. Easter may fall anywhere between 22 March and 25 April.

Table of Regnal Years

	Henry VII
1	22 August 1485 – 21 August 1486
2	22 August 1486 – 21 August 1487
	etc to
24	22 August 1508 – 21 April 1509
	Henry VIII
1	22 April 1509 – 21 April 1510
2	22 April 1510 – 21 April 1511
	etc to
38	22 April 1546 – 28 January 1547
	Edward VI
1	28 January 1547 – 27 January 1548
2	28 January 1548 – 27 January 1549
	etc to
7	28 January 1553 – 6 July 1553
	Jane
1	6 July 1553 – 19 July 1553
	Mary
1	19 July 1553 – 5 July 1554
2	6 July 1554 – 24 July 1554
	Mary with Philip
2&1	25 July 1554 – 5 July 1555
3&1	6 July 1554 – 24 July 1555
3&2	25 July 1555 – 5 July 1556
4&2	6 July 1556 – 24 July 1556
4&3	25 July 1556 – 5 July 1557
5&3	6 July 1557 – 24 July 1557
5&4	25 July 1557 – 5 July 1558
6&4	6 July 1558 – 24 July 1558
6&5	25 July 1558 – 17 November 1558
	Elizabeth
1	17 November 1558 – 16 November 1559
2	17 November 1559 – 16 November 1560
	etc to
45	17 November 1602 – 24 March 1603
	James I (James VI of Scotland from 24 July 1567)
1	24 March 1603 – 23 March 1604
2	24 March 1604 – 23 March 1605
	etc to
23	24 March 1625 – 27 March 1625
	Charles I
1	27 March 1625 – 26 March 1626
2	27 March 1626 – 26 March 1627
	etc to
24	27 March 1626 – 30 January 1649
	The Commonwealth
	31 January 1649 – 28 May 1660
	Charles II
12	29 May 1660 – 29 January 1661
13	30 January 1661 – 29 January 1662
14	30 January 1662 – 29 January 1663
	etc to
37	30 January 1685 – 6 February 1685
	James II
1	6 February 1685 – 5 February 1686
2	6 February 1686 – 5 February 1687
3	6 February 1687 – 5 February 1688
4	6 February 1688 – 11 December 1688
	Interregnum
	12 December 1688 – 12 February 1689
	William and Mary
1	13 February 1689 – 12 February 1690
2	13 February 1690 – 12 February 1691
	etc to
6	13 February 1694 – 27 December 1694
	William III
6	28 December 1694 – 12 February 1695
7	13 February 1695 – 12 February 1696
8	13 February 1696 – 12 February 1697
	etc to
14	13 February 1702 – 8 March 1702
	Anne
1	8 March 1702 – 7 March 1703
2	8 March 1703 – 7 March 1704
	etc to
13	8 March 1714 – 1 August 1714

For example, Henry VIII's reign began on 22 April. His 10th regnal year contained no Easter, because Easter 1518 fell on 4 April, in the 9th year of his reign, and Easter 1519 on 24 April in his 11th year. This contained two Easters, as 8 April 1520 was also within his 11th year. So many moveable feasts are associated with Easter that there is potential for great confusion when documents are dated at Ash Wednesday or Pentecost.

Mary Tudor dated her second year from 6 July 1554, despite her first year beginning on 19 July 1553 following the brief reign of Jane Grey (which Mary ignored for dating purposes); following Mary's own marriage to Philip of Spain an Act of Parliament made him joint monarch from 25 July 1555. For the next three years their joint regnal years dovetail with each other.

During the Commonwealth documents were dated with the year of grace, but regnal years were used again after the Restoration when Charles II dated the first year of his reign from the death of his father. Thus the first English documents dated during his reign, produced in 1660, are dated in his 12th year. The year of grace was again used during the Interregnum in 1688-1689, but William and Mary became joint monarchs on the same day and the confusion of Philip and Mary's regnal years is avoided.

The early modern legal year started on 25 March (known as Lady Day), not 1 January. This is most obvious when looking at parish registers, which although they were primarily religious documents used the legal year, with entries in December, January, February and up to 25 March of one year, then April, May and June of the next. The start of the year was changed by Act of Parliament (Chesterfield's Act) which came into force in 1752 and required the adoption of the Gregorian Calendar. First proposed by Pope Gregory XIII in 1582 to replace the Julian Calendar, which had gradually separated from the solar calendar by ten days during the middle ages, the Gregorian calendar was accepted by most Catholic countries in the late sixteenth century. England retained the Julian Calendar, which meant that its calendar was not only one year behind much of Europe between January and March, but was also ten or eleven days adrift. But even in England the Gregorian practice of dating from 1 January became popular, and for almost two centuries both methods of dating were in operation. English scribes alternated between conventions or wrote both years, in the form 1651/2. In the nineteenth and earlier twentieth centuries the dual date was the usual method of transcription for dates, but from the later twentieth century it has become more common only to provide the modern use.

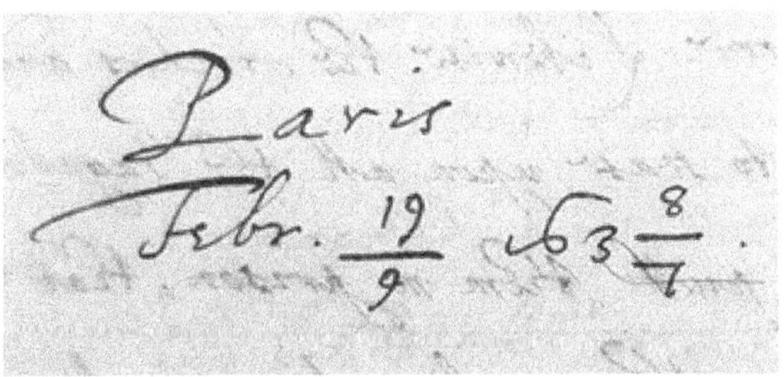
Paris
Febr. 19/9 163 8/7.

A letter written in Paris using the Gregorian calendar on 19 February 1638, French date, to an English recipient for whom the date was 9 February 1637, according to the Julian calendar, TNA SP 78/105

Chesterfield's Act and the adoption of the Gregorian Calendar established the dating of the year from 1 January as standard practice in England and Wales; it had already been adopted in Scotland in 1600. In all three countries it also removed eleven days as 2 September 1752 was followed by 14 September, aligning Britain with most of Europe and making diplomatic and trade related correspondence much simpler.

Divisions of the year are given as months, or in legal documents by the term in which they were created. These terms were of variable length and named after a religious feast close to the date on which they began: Michaelmas Term usually began on 6th October and lasted for around six weeks, Hilary Term for two, three or four weeks from 20 January, Easter Term began on the second Sunday after Easter and lasted for up to four weeks, and Trinity Term began in the first week of July and closed in the final week of the same month. Cheney's *Handbook* provides a ready reckoner to calculate the dates of a term in any given year.

Occasionally scribes adopted the abbreviation of giving the Arabic numeral for the first part of the Latin name of a month, so September was the seventh month in the Roman calendar and abbreviated to 7^{ber}; October, the eight month to 8^{ber}; November, the ninth month to 9^{ber}; and December the tenth month to 10^{ber}. To make matters even more confusing the scribe might employ Roman numerals for part of the date.

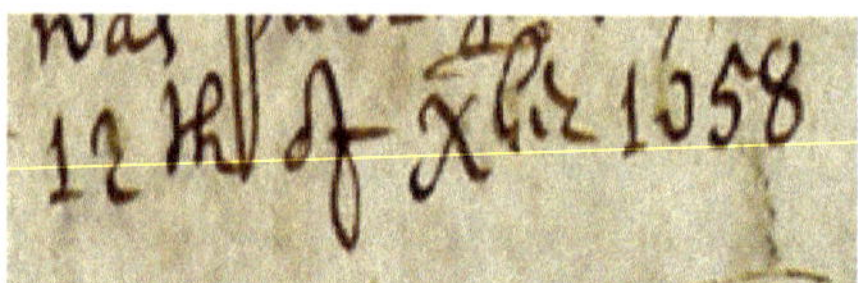

12th of X^{ber} 1658 – the 12th of December 1658

Days might be expressed in relation to a religious feast: for example, the Monday after Pentecost or the Wednesday before Michaelmas. Tables for calculating these dates are given in Cheney's *Handbook* together with lists of leap years, the dates of Easter and much more besides. Days, when expressed numerically as days of the month, may be presumed to be in their Latin form, so the abbreviation for the first day would not be 1st but 1° for *primo*, the second would not be 2nd but 2do for *secundo*, and so on. When numbers are abbreviated in an English, rather than a Latin, form it is common for the abbreviation to be for a reversed form of the date: the two and twentieth day would be abbreviated to the 22th rather than the 22nd, the three and twentieth to the 23th, and so on.

Certain days appear regularly in Tudor and Stuart documents because they were the traditional days when rents were paid and courts were held. Foremost are the quarter-days: Michaelmas (29 September), Christmas (25 December), the Annunciation of the Virgin Mary, usually called Lady Day (25 March), and the Nativity of St John the Baptist (24 June); but there are numerous other days, such as Hock day (the 2nd Sunday after Easter), Pentecost (the 7th Sunday after Easter), St Peter ad Vincula, also known as Lammas (1 August), and Martinmas (11 November) which marked the beginning or end of phases in the agricultural year.

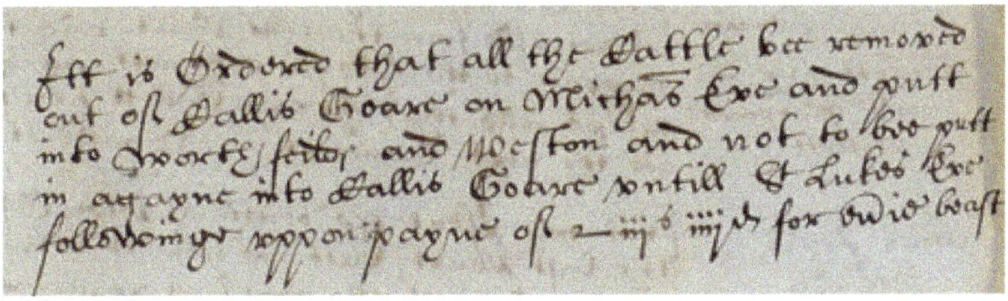

Itt is Ordered that all the Cattle bee removed out of Callis Goare on Micha[elma]s Eve and putt into Worth feilds and Weston and not to bee putt in agayne into Callis Goare untill St Lukes Eve followinge uppon payne of iijs iiijd for ev[er]ie beast [Michaelmas - 29 September, St Luke the Evangelist's Day - 18 October] Worth Matravers manor court presentment, 1632

From the middle of the seventeenth century there was a special dating system used in Quaker documents. Quakers would not use pagan names for days or months so they gave them numbers instead. The first day was Sunday, often represented as the 1st day, day 1 or just as 1, the second was Monday, and so on. So if an event was planned for the third Wednesday of the following month it would be represented as 'the third 4d of next month'. Similarly the months were numbered: the first was March, the second was April, and so on. So a Quaker date 1699.5.16 was 16 July 1699, 1699.5.12 was 12 July 1699. Before 1752, while the rest of the country began their year on 25 March, the Quakers chose 1 March as the start of the year, so 1700.11.2 was 2 January 1701, but 1700.3.5 was 5 March 1700. This problem was removed from 1 January 1752 when Quakers joined with the rest of the country and January became their first month.

There are many other aspects to dating in documents which are too specialist for this volume; Orthodox, Jewish and Muslim calendars were used by members of those faiths. When interpreting dates, along with many other aspects of sixteenth and seventeenth century writing, it is always worth remembering that the scribe was following a system that was clear to himself and his contemporaries. There is no secret to the code and no intention to confuse the reader, just a different method of expression.

Ligatures and contractions

In an age before shorthand or typing, economy in writing was achieved by using ligatures and standard abbreviations or contractions. These are often unfamiliar to the modern reader and are easiest to identify by following the course of the writing as the scribe found a path to keep the quill on the parchment or paper.

The most common ligatures are 'ch', 'sh' and 'th', often found superscript at the end of words, and 'st', 'ss' and 'ff' more frequently found in the middle of words.

ch

sh

th

st

ss

ff

Note that a common form of the ‘ss’ ligature consisted of a long ‘s’ dropping below the line followed by a short ‘s’. These letters are easy to identify in isolation, but more difficult when embedded in a text.

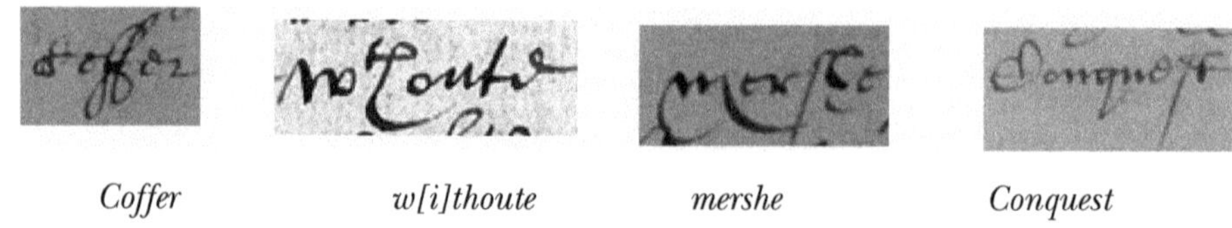

Coffer *w[i]thoute* *mershe* *Conquest*

Secretary, Italic and Court hands were peppered with abbreviations throughout the sixteenth and seventeenth centuries. Usually they derive from medieval contractions and a few have survived into the 21st century. Readers will be familiar with Mr, Mrs, Revd, and esq., and the abbreviated Latin etc (*et cetera*, meaning *and other things*), viz (*videlicet*, meaning *namely*) and sic (*sic.* meaning *thus*, as in *sic erat scriptum*, thus it has been written), but there were many more and a number of standard abbreviations attached to particular letters.

The letter with which contractions are most associated is ‘p’. In *p + vowel + r* combinations a series of different signs indicated the omission of the letters including ‘*ar*’, ‘*or*’, ‘*re*’ and ‘*ro*’ in words such as p[ar]ish or p[ro]test. Different forms of contraction represented the omission of different letters.

When ‘*p*’ is followed by a vowel and then ‘*r*’ the omission is shown by a horizontal line through the descender of the ‘*p*’ or by an upward curve coming backwards from the base of the descender and turning to pass through the descender below the line.

In the case of ‘p’ followed by ‘r’ and then a vowel different forms were employed:

However, many writers, through carelessness, laziness or lack of training , did not use these precisely defined forms and instead adopted an all purpose contraction mark for all these 'p' + two other letter combinations. This is usually the first example given above. In these cases the exact combination of letters will only become clear from the sense and context of the word: prison, person and parson could be visually indistinguishable in such circumstances.

Whether the scribe formed their contraction according to the established precedents or used a universal contraction, the greatest difficulty in recognising a ‘p’ abbreviation is identifying what has been written in the context of a text with closely associated letters on the same line and the line below.

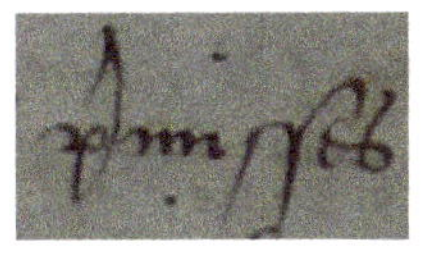
P[re]misses

p[re]misses

counterp[ar]t

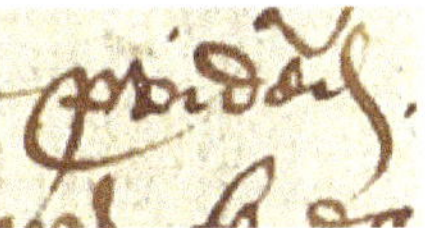
p[ro]vided

After the 'p' contractions the most common specific forms are the 'er' or ur' forms, often represented by a stroke that resembles a superscript 'r' or a flick returning over the preceding letter.

deliv[er]ed

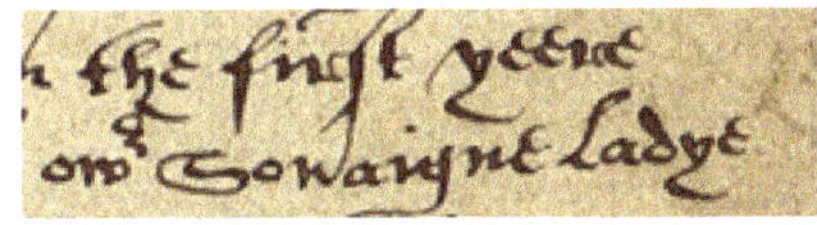
ow[ur] Sov[er]aigne Ladye

Another medieval contraction which persisted well into the sixteenth century, although rarely into the seventeenth, is for 'ser'. This takes the form of a long 's' with a curved line crossing the tail. It is usually employed at the beginning of a word and is much more difficult to distinguish when in the middle surrounded by other letters.

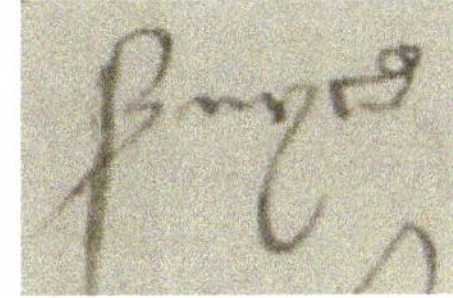
S[er]vyce

P[re]s[er]ve

Other contractions with specific meanings are less common. The letter 'X' is used at the beginning of names like Christopher or Christina in place of the first element 'Christ' and the medieval contraction for the common Latin ending 'rum' is sometimes found at the end of words.

Sarum

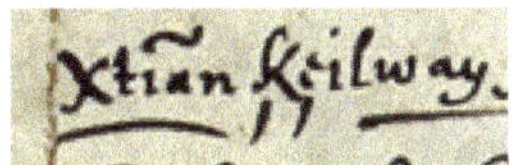
Christian Keilway

A general contraction stroke of a line above a word was commonly employed to indicate the omission of one or more letters. Frequently these letters are 'm', 'n' or 'u' particularly when they appear in a series of minims.

An[n]o 1582

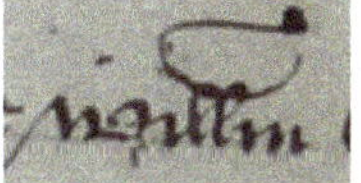
Will[ia]m

dec[eas]ed

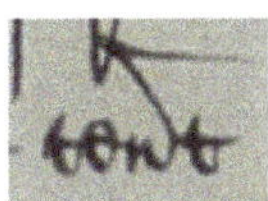
Ten[emen]t

Contractions are always more difficult when viewed in combination, but they are usually used consistently. A reader who is familiar with the set of contractions used by one scribe will not find it too difficult to recognise those used by another employing the same hand.

w[i]t[h] thapp[ur]t[e]n[a]nc[es]

This final example is particularly tricky. The scribe probably pronounced 'with' as 'wit' and did not intend to include an 'h'; running the definite article into a word beginning with a vowel was common; the 'ur' contraction is standard, yet there is no indication that later vowels have been omitted; and the looped stroke at the end, which resembles a 'p' with a forward tail for a descender, is a standard way of indicating 'es' at the end of a word. It looks almost impossible in isolation, but in context it makes immediate sense and could be nothing else.

Christian names

Christian names were commonly abbreviated, particularly in parish registers, manorial documents and taxation returns. As there was such a small pool of male Christian names it was often unnecessary to repeat them in full. Most are obvious: Chas for Charles, Ric for Richard. A few may be confusing: Jo, Jno or Joh are always John while Jos is Joseph, Xpher is Christopher. Some have several forms Hen or Hy for Henry, Jas for James (never Jason) but also Jac, short for the Latin form of James, *Jacobus*, may also be used.

Occasionally, a scribe writing in English may use a Latin form of a Christian name: Dionysius for Dennis, Egidius for Giles, Agneta for Agnes or Cecilia for Cecily. Several genealogy websites give lists of these names for which the English form is not always obvious.

Women's names were much more numerous and changed as they were perceived to be fashionable or archaic. Eliz for Elizabeth, My for Mary and Marg for Margaret are among the most common. Beware the unfamiliar: names like Ames, Avice and Emmott might appear to be mistakes, diminutives or abbreviations but they are actual names used in the sixteenth century.

Yogh and *Thorn*; two obsolete letters

In addition to the letters in the modern alphabet Anglo-Saxon scribes employed three extra characters known as *edh*, *yogh* and *thorn*. The character *edh*, which represented the sound 'th' in 'this' or 'then' had passed out of use shortly after the Conquest, but *yogh* persisted into the sixteenth century and *thorn* into the nineteenth century.

Yogh was written to resemble a 'z' with a tail, ȝ, and might be pronounced as a guttural 'gh' ȝat (gate) or wrouȝt (wrought), a strong 'y' in ȝet (yet) or a hard 'th' in ȝee (thee) or ȝine (thine). Medieval pronunciation shifts have led to the *-burȝ* place name element becoming Salis*bury* and Edin*burgh*. The letter *yogh* persisted into the sixteenth century, particularly in northern counties, but it was not included in most printing character sets and had fallen out of use by the seventeenth century.

Thorn was a much more significant letter in the sixteenth and seventeenth centuries as it stood for the common sound and letter pairing 'th'. Thorn was originally written to resemble the letter 'y' but, from the medieval period a second common form resembled a combined 'b' and 'p' with both an ascender and a descender þ.

By the sixteenth century *thorn* was increasingly written as a 'y' and therein lies the source of much confusion. The form (*thorn* + other letters) e.g. þ^{m} (them) or þ^{t} (that) became much closer, visually, to *ym* or *yt* even though these words had always been pronounced *them* and *that*. By the seventeenth century thorn as a separate letter was no longer used. This was probably because like yogh it was not included in printers' character sets, but people continued to substitute the letter 'y'. It is this that has given rise to the notorious and absurd non-word *Ye* meaning 'The', as in *Ye olde teashoppe*. In the past *thorn* was occasionally transcribed as 'y' but this is now considered an error and the *thorn* letter, however it is expressed in a text, should always be transcribed as 'th'.

þ^{m} would always be transcribed *th[e]m*, þ^{t} as *th[a]t* and þ^{e} as *the*
and therefore
y^{m} would always be transcribed *th[e]m*, *y*^{t} as *th[a]t* and *y*^{e} as *the*

Transcription

Styles of transcription vary depending upon how the resulting text will be used. Most county record societies and journals will have a set of guidelines which provide a house style and ensure consistency between editors. If in doubt, or if transcribing for a website or a local society, there are several publications recommended in the bibliography.

The style of transcription used in this volume is intended to illustrate which different hands have been used and in particular to highlight the omission of letters and use of abbreviations by placing them in square brackets [thus]. For most publications the expansion of words is silent, and takes place without indicating that certain letters have been omitted. Where they are significant in understanding the text superscript letters and interlineated words may be represented by superscript letters ^{thus}, but for most transcripts standard letters would be used. Similarly words that have been struck through may be shown ~~thus~~ when they are significant, while in most transcripts a word that had been struck though as a simple error might be omitted. Round brackets have been used for explanatory notes on the text (thus), but kept to a minimum as they interfere with the flow of the text and where possible this information is best placed in a footnote or end notes. Translations from other languages are given in italics with the original within round brackets: *Firstly* (Latin: *Primo*).

No additional punctuation has been added to the texts in this volume. Although this makes some passages difficult to read it avoids the reader having to work out what has been added. Most transcribers will introduce a minimal amount of punctuation to assist the reader, making clear in their introduction that they have done so. Similarly all capitalisation has been reproduced from the texts. This is not always easy, as some scribes used slightly enlarged forms of small letters as capitals, and at times the intended form is not clear. It is generally the case that writers in the past used more capitals than we do today, and a faithfully reproduced text may not flow very easily for a modern reader, so some transcribers will chose to follow a modern convention for the use of capitals. This is a reasonable approach, but must be applied consistently, stated in the introduction to the transcription and, if intended for publication, be carried out with the agreement of the journal editor.

Rules and conventions for transcribing

There are various rules for transcribing. Some are overarching principles which should always be followed. Others depend upon the conventions of a publication or series. For instance academic publishers may require all words to be transcribed exactly as they appear in a text, because the range of readers cannot be anticipated and a faithful reproduction is the most appropriate form. But a transcriber reproducing parish registers for a website may decide to modernise forenames for convenience and to avoid confusion. This is a legitimate approach, but if such editorial decisions are made the transcriber must inform the reader of what has been done in an introduction and indicate in the text any sections which are uncertain.

The most important rule is to be consistent. Whether or not using an established set of conventions it is necessary to follow the same set of rules throughout the text. Inform the reader of what practice is being followed. Indicate whether punctuation has been added, capitalisation modernised or Roman numerals converted to Arabic. The reader should not be in doubt about, or have to guess, the relationship of the transcript to the text.

It is likely that some words cannot be transcribed. In any hand some of the text may be illegible, poorly written, covered by ink blots, bound in a margin, or torn from an edge. Indicate to the reader that this is the case by the use of a footnote, endnote or an insertion in square brackets such as [*illegible word*] or [*torn margin, several words lost*]. It is useful to indicate why the text cannot be transcribed, because readers may want to revisit the text: a missing section will always be missing, but another reader may be able to interpret an illegible word or use photographic enhancement to read a smudged section.

It is essential not to guess a word or section that cannot be read. Leaving a gap or putting a bracketed question mark is honest and appreciated by the reader. An incorrect guess is simply wrong and potentially very misleading.

It is always worth seeking a second opinion. A word presented to another researcher or an archivist might be recognised immediately – this is not because they are necessarily better at reading the text but, much like a crossword, one transcriber can puzzle over a single word or section and not see the wood for the trees. Transcribing in groups or pairs is a method used by many academic projects whereby researchers,working on different texts from the same period and group of documents, are available to help each other with difficult sections.

There are different levels of transcription. The choice of method is usually determined by the eventual purpose of the exercise. A transcript for an academic paper, county record society or postgraduate dissertation will probably need to be completed according to a defined set of rules. For publications of a less specialist nature, or where transcripts are seldom included, a magazine or website editor may rely upon the transcriber to set their own parameters.

At the start of a project the following options may be considered:

- Preparing a text that is identical to the original in all aspects including spelling, punctuation and capitalisation and using symbols, abbreviations and contraction marks to mimic those used by the scribe. In the late eighteenth and nineteenth centuries a typeface, known as Record Type, was used to recreate the appearance of some handwritten texts.

TERRA ARCHIEPI CANTVAR. *IN WALETONE HVND.*
II. ARCHIEPS Lanfranc ten in dn̄io *CROINDENE* . T.R.E. ſe
defd ꝑ quat xx . hid . 7 modo ꝑ . xvi . hid 7 una v . Tra . ē
.xx . car . In dn̄io ſunt . iiii . car̄ . 7 xlviii . uitti 7 xxv . bord . cū
.xxxiiii . car . Ibi æccla . 7 un̄ molin̄ de . v . ſol . 7 viii . ac pti . Silua
de . cc . porc.
De tra huj m ten Reſtold vii . hid de archiepo . Radulf . i . hidā.
7 inde hn̄t . vii . lib̄ 7 viii . ſol . de gablo.

A section of Domesday book reproduced in Record Type

- Preparing a text that is identical to the original in all aspects including spelling, punctuation and capitalisation, and indicating by the use of square brackets where letters have been inserted, abbreviations expanded and punctuation added. This is the most difficult approach as the transcriber not only needs to be able to recognise a word, but also to be certain of how the scribe intended it to be written and the meaning of all abbreviations. This sort of transcript may be useful for academics, but it is more difficult for the general reader.
- Preparing a text which involves some degree of modernisation, for example by inserting punctuation to make the sense clearer, using modern capitalisation to make it easier to read, and expanding abbreviations and contractions silently, without the use of square brackets or superscript letters.
- Preparing a text which changes the character of the original, by modernisation of spelling and punctuation, translation of Latin sections, or standardisation of variant spellings and forenames, while retaining, for example, the original word order. This involves a considerable degree of editorial input and the transcriber must make it absolutely clear what changes they have made. This approach will not satisfy every reader – some may need to refer back to the original – but the great majority will find this the easiest form of text to read and, as long as the transcriber clearly sets out what changes they have made, one of the most useful.
- Finally, a text may be revised by restructuring the original so it becomes a paraphrase or calendar. This approach might be used in particularly repetitive texts where a lengthy introductory passage or formula need only be reproduced once. For instance:

At the day and time aforesaid Paul Rogers came and swore upon his oath that the following statement is in all manner and form true and accurate
At the day and time aforesaid Andrew Fraser came and swore upon his oath that the following statement is in all manner and form true and accurate

At the day and time aforesaid Simon Kirke came and swore upon his oath that the following statement is in all manner and form true and accurate

might become:

At the day and time aforesaid Paul Rogers came and swore upon his oath that the following statement is in all manner and form true and accurate
The same day Andrew Fraser swore
The same day Simon Kirke swore

Again, the introduction needs to state that repetitive entries have been calendared.

Each approach is valid in some circumstances, but different approaches should not be mixed in the same piece of work. The criteria should be established at the start and applied all the way through the transcription. If the form wth is used at the start it should not suddenly become *w[i]th* halfway through. A useful approach is to read the entire text before beginning to transcribe. This will not only make the identification of awkward sections easier, but also help to determine what approach to transcription is used.

Recently it has become common to expand abbreviations and also to note ambiguities in the original text. These may result from a fold, tear, ink blot or water damage making all or part of a word indecipherable. In these circumstances it is reasonable to guess what the word might be as long as it is clear to the reader that this has been done. The following conventions may act as a guide for those who are not following the established editorial practices of a series:

[ ] expanded abbreviations may be enclosed in square brackets, and all such expansions indicated in the same way, even when there are several within the same word, for example:

> $w^{th}n$ may be transcribed as *w[i]th[i]n*
> *co'on* may be transcribed as *com[m]on*

/ or // may be used to show the end of a line in an original text, especially if the transcript is not laid out in the same form as the original. It is a particularly useful to identify the end of a line if a transcription is accompanied by a modernised version as it enables the reader to move between the two more easily.

> horses is now by reason therof become Lame and / unable to Gett his
> Living or stirr abroad but/ Lyes almost bedd rotten, in the house of one/

<word> may be used to indicate that a word has been deleted from the original text. If the original is legible then ~~strike through~~ might be preferred, but this convention remains useful for documents with many illegible words.

> Although they have been <dayly> importuned
> Although they have been ~~dayly~~ importuned
> Although they have been <~~dayly~~> importuned

\word/ may be used to indicate that a word has been interlineated or inserted into the original text (for example, a phrase added later between two lines of text. Other symbols that might be used are /word/ or ^word . In this volume ^{superscript} has been used. This has the advantage of being visually closer to the original, but the disadvantage of being more difficult to read.

20 years last past \about two years since/ made address unto
20 years last past about two years since made address unto
20 years last past /about two years since/ made address unto
20 years last past about two years since made address unto

[?] may be used to indicate that a word is possible rather than definite; the question mark in brackets can be placed immediately before the word or number, or the word can be included within the square brackets.
[?]tenement
[?tenement]

[...] may be used to show that a section of text is missing, through damage or defacement; or alternatively the form [*text damaged*] or similar can be used.
Was s[er]vant unto Will[ia]m Fazakerley gent[leman] & [*text damaged*] the Castle of Liverpoole.
Was s[er]vant unto Will[ia]m Fazakerley gent[leman] & [...] the Castle of Liverpoole.

There are numerous other conventions, some highly technical, and it is important to note that individual editors might well employ their own, non-standard symbols and styles. The crucial point is to make clear to the reader all the rules and conventions, symbols and methods that have been used.

Select Bibliography

Dates

C.R. Cheney and M. Jones, *Handbook of Dates: For Students of British History*, 2nd edition (Royal Historical Society Guides and Handbooks, 2000).
V. Norrington, 'The First Month called March: the Dating of Quaker documents' in *Suffolk Review.* New Series 27 (1996).

Editing texts

P. D. A. Harvey, *Editing Historical Records* (British Library, 2001)
R. F. Hunnisett, *Editing Records for Publication* (British Records Association, 1977).

Latin

E. A. Gooder, *Latin for Local Historians, an introduction* (Longman, 1978).
D. Stuart, *Latin for Local and Family Historians* (Phillimore, 2002).

Palaeography

H. Grieve, *Examples of English Handwriting, 1150-1750* (Essex R.O., 1954)
L. C. Hector, *The Handwriting of English Documents*, 2nd ed. (Dorking, 1966).
H. Marshall, *Palaeography for Family and Local Historians* (Phillimore, 1999)

Sources and Guides

N. Alcock, *Old Title Deeds: A Guide for Local and Family Historians* (Phillimore, 1986)
C. Chapman, *How Heavy, How Much and How Long?: Weights, Money and Other Measures Used by Our Ancestors* (Chapman's Records Cameos, 1995)
M. Jurkowski, C. L. Smith and D. Crook, *Lay Taxes in England and Wales, 1188-1688* (Public Records Office, 1998).
D. Stuart, *Manorial Records* (Chichester, 1992).
W. E. Tate, *The Parish Chest: a Study of the Records of Parochial Administration in England*, 3rd edition (Cambridge, 1969).

Several local and family history societies publish short pamphlet guides to records. Foremost are the series of guides produced by the Family History Federation which introduce a wide range of record types.

Palaeography summer schools are run by several English Universities and online tutorial courses in reading Tudor and Stuart handwriting, providing further examples of texts, may be found on the National Archives, Cambridge University and Bodleian Library websites among others:
http://www.nationalarchives.gov.uk/palaeography/
https://www.english.cam.ac.uk/ceres/ehoc/
http://rycote.bodleian.ox.ac.uk/palaeography

The Texts

The texts used in this edition have been selected from across the sixteenth and seventeenth centuries and from a range of English counties and archives. They are representative texts of the sort that the researcher might encounter when studying local history and none has been chosen because they are particularly difficult or obscure.

They have been arranged in reverse chronological order to demonstrate the development of handwriting over the two hundred years covered by this guide. Nevertheless, it is important to note that some employ archaic features, while others are quite fashionable or advanced for their time. There is not a simple linear progression, but a gradual shift towards new styles in different areas, at different times, usually led from London and the south-east.

The range of documents is described below to provide context since it is strongly recommended that researchers understand the background to particular types or classes of document. Guides to some records are listed in the bibliography.

Family, estate and manorial documents

Estate accounts, surveys, manorial court records and stewards' papers are some of the most commonly used documents available to local historians. They are found in family and estate collections in county archives, or still in private collections, as well as in the National Archives having either been made for Crown lands or presented in legal cases.

Typically these accounts are divided into income and expenses; they include local, technical and dialect terms and may contain a mixture of Arabic and Roman numerals. The more detailed accounts may enable the researcher to trace the expenses incurred during the farming year which indicate the dates of different agrarian activities and hiring of casual labour.

Private correspondence can include some of the most difficult and most rewarding documents. These texts are often written quickly and with less concern for neatness than many official records, and when they contain technical terms there may be insufficient context to establish their meaning. All these problems aside, these are the documents that give some of the deepest insights into the character and concerns of people in the past.

Examples in this guide are:

- Oxfordshire love letter, 1652.
- Account book of Hengrave Park, Suffolk, 1587.
- Survey of Kettering manor, Northamptonshire, 1585.
- Survey of the manor of Compton Dundon, Somerset.
- Letter from Hugh Parker to his father James Parker, Lancashire, *circa* 1509.

- Steward's papers relating to the Devon lands of Sir Thomas Kitson of Hengrave, 1580.
- A letter from the Abbot of Cerne, Dorset.
- Letter regarding the manor of Halsway, Somerset.
- Abstract of the expences at Chiswick, Middlesex, 1680.

Legal and Local Government Records

At a local level, manor, borough and hundred courts dealt with minor issues and passed relatively minor sentences. The records of these courts are often found in borough, family and estate collections within county archives.

The Quarter Sessions were courts held in each county four times each year at Hilary (or Epiphany), Easter, Trinity (or Midsummer) and Michaelmas terms from 1388 to 1972. They were established for cases that could not be resolved at the local hundred courts, but were not serious enough to be brought to the Assizes. The Quarter Sessions rolls are public records and are held in county archives where they are exploited by local historians studying subjects as various as vagrancy, bastardy, petty crime, turnpikes and railways. Family historians may be drawn to the long lists of names in land tax returns and of those qualified to serve as jurors as well as individual case records.

Final concords, or final agreements, are one of several series of documents for which deliberately archaic hands continued to be used into the nineteenth century. Clerks in central courts such as the Court of Common Pleas, Court of King's Bench, Chancery and in some probate offices were trained in this style. Originally this had been the medieval court hand, but over the years it became stylised and exaggerated.

Agreements were created by central courts, such as the Court of Common Pleas, as indented copies: the same text was written on three parts of a piece of parchment which was then cut with a wavy line between the sections. The copies held by the parties could be verified by matching them to each other or to the copy held by the Court of Common Pleas. The copies retained by the court form a large series of documents at the National Archives, but those held in family and estate collections in county archives are often more useful because they tend to be retained with other title deeds for the same property.

Records of the assizes, Exchequer, Chancery, Court of Kings Bench, Admiralty and a number of other specialist courts are held at the National Archives, although the writs, judgements and declarations that they issues find their way into many other collections.

Taxation records are a useful source for local and family historians and a good starting point for those learning new hands. These long lists provide familiar forenames, often repeated, which give the transcriber the chance to encounter a large number of capital letters which appear infrequently in other texts. By transcribing the forenames first the researcher learns both the hand and the individual quirks of the scribe before moving on to the surnames.

Taxation assessments are often used by family and local historians to place individuals in a community, or to measure wealth, population growth or density.

The Exchequer required that assessments and accounts, often naming individual taxpayers, were returned to their central offices in Westminster where they were scrutinised by auditors. These documents survive in very large numbers, but care should be taken in making comparisons between them as the basis of assessment often changed from one tax to the next. Most taxation documents are held in the National Archives in the E179 class, but a few may be found in borough collections and the family collections of those gentlemen appointed as collectors.

Examples in this guide are:

- Petition of the inhabitants of East Harnham, Wiltshire, to the Quarter Sessions, Hilary term, 1673.
- Deposition concerning a theft at Longbridge Deverill, Wiltshire, presented at Quarter Sessions, Trinity term 1671.
- Presentment of the constables of Calne borough to the Quarter Sessions, Devizes, Wiltshire, Easter term 1612.
- Final Concord, relating to lands in Broadway, Upway and Nottington, Dorset, 1653.
- Quarter Sessions, Calendar of the house of Correction, Dorset, 1629.
- Lay subsidy assessment, part of Brownsall hundred, Dorset, 1628.
- Somerset case in the Court of Requests, January 1523.
- Hearth tax assessment, Lincolnshire, 1664.
- Hearth tax exemption certificates, Monmouthshire, 1664.

Church records

The parish chest formerly contained many records besides the registers used by family historians and demographers. Overseers' accounts provide evidence of poor relief, highway maintenance, expenditure on the fabric of the church and a range of other local matters. Incumbents commented on all manner of social issues as well as their own circumstances; and church courts, whose records survive in diocesan archives, cast judgements on a wide range of social and moral issues.

It is useful to note that from 1598 at least until the beginning of civil registration in 1837 parish priests and churchwardens were obliged to send a copy of their parish registers to the bishop. Known as bishops' transcripts, these may survive from an earlier date than the parish registers. Most were carefully copied, but inevitably there are some contemporary transcription errors and the parish copy, where it survives, should be regarded as definitive. Bishops' transcripts are kept in the diocesan archive.

Until 1858 probate was administered through church courts and wills, administrations, inventories and registers are found among the church records. The Preogative Courts of Canterbury and York proved the wills of wealthier people who held property in more than one county, these records are at the National Archives, while most people proved their wills in their local consistory or archdeaconry courts.

Church record keeping has always been better than that of many other institutions, and the requirement of churches to have locked chests meant that they sometimes became used as repositories by members of their congregations.

Each diocese appoints one or more repositories, usually county record offices, to be the place of deposit for documents covered by the Parochial Registers and Records Measure, 1978, which are deposited there by the parishes. Some are centralised in a single archive along with the diocesan records, including most church court proceedings, while others are divided between several archives in different archdeaconries. For instance, in the diocese of Salisbury the parish and archdeaconry records are divided between the Dorset History Centre, the Berkshire Record Office, and the Wiltshire and Swindon History Centre. The latter also maintains the records of diocesan administration such as church courts and bishops' registers.

Examples in this guide are:

- The parish register of Brightwell Baldwin, Oxfordshire, 1598-1605.
- Churchwardens' Account, Sherborne, Dorset, 1548.
- Glebe terrier of Dalham, Suffolk, 1613.
- Letter of Juell Longe to the official of the bishop of Salisbury, undated, probably 1612,
- Will of Bastian Bord, Henley, Oxfordshire, 1584.
- Bishop's visitation, deanery of Avebury, Avebury and Alton Priors, Wiltshire, 1553,
- Licence for a Gillingham parishioner to eat meat during Lent, 1595.

Some of these texts are more difficult to read, others more difficult to interpret, but all provide an insight into life in the sixteenth and seventeenth century that can be accessed with a little patience and some practice.

Examples

May 1680. An Abstract of the Expences at Chiswick in the month of May 1680

			li	s	d
Butchers meat	Beefe 930 lb at about 3d ob lb	11:17:05			
	Mutton and Veale 770½ lb at about 4d	12:19:09			
	Lambe ½ a case	00:05:04			
	Neats Tongues 3	00:05:04			
	Sweetbreads 2 at 6d	00:01:00			
	Marrowbones 12 at 6d	00:06:00	26	06	00
	Calvesheads 5	00:08:08			
	Lambstones 2 pe at 4d	00:00:08			
	Sheeps head	00:00:06			
	Calfesgether	00:01:04			
Poultry	Pulletts gr. 20 at 2s 4d	02:06:08			
	Chicks 86	02:13:08			
	Pigeons 12	00:02:09			
	Rabbetts 22 at 11d	01:00:02	8	18	03
	Turkey Chicks 16 at 2s 6d	02:00:00			
	Phesant ta:	00:06:00			
	Greene Geese 2 at 2s 6d	00:05:00			
	Pigeons ta: 4 at 12d	00:04:00			
Fish	Soales 7 pe	00:13:00			
	Maquerills 34	01:12:10			
	Lobsters 3	00:03:00			
	Salt fish 3	00:07:00	4	07	10
	Flounders	00:11:06			
	Carps 3	00:14:00			
	Smelts	00:04:06			
Beer & Wine 7. 2. 0	Beer 20 barrells at 6s 9d per bar.	06:15:00	7	02	00
	White wine 6 bottles at 14d	00:07:00			

Household Expenses of Sir Stephen Fox, 1680

May 1680	An Abstract of the Expences at Chiswick in the month of May 1680		
	Beefe 930^{lb} at about 3^{d} p[er]^{lb}	11:17:05	
	Mutton and Veale $770½^{lb}$ at about 4^{d}	12:19:09	
	Lambe ½ a case	00:05:04	
Butchers meat	Neats Tongues 3	00:05:04	£ s d
	Sweetbreads 2 at 6^{d}	00:01:00	26 06 00
	Marrowbones 12 at 6^{d}	00:06:00	
	Calvesheads 5	00:08:08	
	Lambstones 2 p[ai]r at 4^{d}	00:00:08	
	Sheeps head	00:00:06	
	Calfesgether	00:01:04	
	Pulletts gr. 20 at 2^{s} 4^{d} 2	02:06:08	
	Chicks 86	02:13:08	
Poultry	Pigeons 12	00:02:09	
	Rabbetts 22 at 11d	01:00:02	8 18 03
	Turkey Chicks 16 at 2^{s} 6^{d}	02:00:00	
	Pheasant ea[ch]:	00:06:00	
	Greene Geese 2 at 2^{s} 6^{d}	00:05:00	
	Pigeons ea[ch]: 4 at 12^{d}	00:04:00	
	Soales 7 p[ai]r	00:13:00	
	Maquerills 34	01:12:10	
	Lobsters 3	00:05:00	
Fish	Salt fish 3	00:07:00	4 07 10
	Flounders	00:11:06	
	Carps 5	00:14:00	
	Smelts	00:04:06	
Beer & Wine	Beer 20 barrells at 6^{s} 9^{d} p[er] bar[re]^{ll}	06:15:00	
7. 2. 0	White wine 6 bottles at 14^{d}	00:07:00	7 02 00

A clear italic hand of the later seventeenth century.

The words, spellings, weights, measures and currency may all be unfamiliar, but a list of people, places, produce or purchases is a good way to start reading documents from a new period. The sense of the whole document is clear.

Many of the letter forms in this document have features that are typical of sixteenth and seventeenth century hands:

It is difficult to distinguish between some common letters: capital 'F' in Flounders is only distinguished from capital 'T' in Turkey by a very small cross stroke.

Some letters unexpectedly drop below the line, here capital 'C'.

Ascending upright elements of lower case 'b', 'd', 'h', 'k' and 'l' have exaggerated loops which may become as large as the lower part of the letters.

Line 13, the abbreviation 'gr.' may be for 'grown' but as this is uncertain it has been left unexpanded.

To the Honorable the Bench /

The Humble petition of the Inhabitants
of the Hamblett of East Harnham within
/ the parish of Britford /

Humbly sheweing unto your Worpps: that whereas the
said Hamblett of East Harnham is now
much burdned with the poore of the same place
by reason of the many widdowes & fatherlesse
Children with others the poore that depende
wholy upon releife the request of the said
Inhabitants (your Worpps: poore petitioners is)
that according to your accustomed Clemencie)
you would be pleased to order the said parish
of Britford to Joyne with the said Hamblett in
order to a collection for and towards the reliefe
of the said poore and your petitioners shall as
by dutie stand bounde to pray for
your Worpps: longe live
/ and happines /

John Pallmer
Ouer Seer
Artur Burges
Joseph Bates

110

Petition of the inhabitants of East Harnham, Wiltshire, to the Quarter Sessions, Hilary term 1673

To the Honorable the Bench /

The Humble petic[i]on of the Inhabitants
of the Hamblett of East Harnham w[i]th in -
/ the p[ar]ish of Britford. /

Humbly shewing unto your Wor[shi]ps that whereas the
said Hamblett of East Harnham is now -
much burdened w[i]th the poore of the same place
by reason of the many widdowes & fatherlesse
Children w[i]th others the poore that depends -
wholy upon releife the request of the said
Inhabitants / your Wor[shi]ps poore petic[i]oners is,
(that according to your accustomed Clementcie)
you would be pleased to order the said p[ar]ish
of Britford to Joyne w[i]th the said Hamblett in -
order to acoletion for and twowards the releife
of the said poore and your petic[i]oners shall as
by dutie stand bound to pray for

Your Wor[shi]ps longe lives
/ and happines /

John Pallmer
Over Seear
Artur Burges
Joseph Bates

This is a typical hand of the late seventeenth century.

The initial letter of 'humbly' (line 5) is poorly formed, but can only be an 'h'.

The words 'a' and 'collection' are run together to form 'acolection' (line 15).

The contraction of petic[i]on (line 20) and your (line 5) hardly seems worth the effort, while Wor[shi]ps is clearly a standard abbreviation used in this jurisdiction.

The flat bottomed 'r' and long 's' in *reason* (line 8) and the leading ascender for the 'u' in *upon* (line 10) are among the more testing letters. Note also the different forms of terminal 's' in *is* (line 11), *as* (line 16), *lives* (line 18) and *happines* (line 19).

We who subscribe doe hereby certify and declare to all whom it may concerne That Joseph Deberlinus of Newport is a very poore man and not any way able to pay the money on him imposed for the two ffireharthes in his now dwelling house in Newport aforesaid according to the Act of Parliament in that case provided. Witnes our hands hereto this twenty seaventh day of June 1664.

Thomas Champion Henry Skardon

Matthias Goldsmith minist

Wee who subscribe doe hereby certify and declare to all whome it may concerne that Simon Russell is a poore man and unable to pay the money on him imposed for the seaverall hearths in his now dwelling house in Newport In witnes whereof wee have hereunto sett our hands the 29th of June Anno Dni 1664.

This is to satifie to home this may consarne that henerey Milds of Nuport is a verrey poore man and not abell to pay the harth mony witnest our handes this prasent day of June 1664

Thomas Champion Henry Skardon

Robart Post Colecter Matt: Goldsmith minist

PUBLIC RECORD OFFICE

Three Hearth Tax Exemption Certificates from Monmouthshire, 1664

Three exemption certificates for the hearth tax, Newport, Monmouthshire, 1664

Certificate 1

We who subscribe doe hereby certify and declare to all whome it
may Concerne That Joseph Dabertine of Newport is a very poore man
and not any way able to pay the money on him imposed for the two
firehearths in his now dwelling howse in Newport aforesaid according
to the Act of Parliam[en]t in that case provided, Witnes our hands hereto
this twenty seaventh day of June 1664
Thomas Champion Church Warden
Matthias Goldsmith minist[er]

Certificate 2

Wee who subscribe doe hereby certify and declare
to all whome it may concerne that Simon Russell
is apoore man and not able to pay the money on him
imposed for the seaverall hearths in his now
dwelling howse in Newport In witnes whereof
wee have hereunto sett our hands the 29th of June
Anno D[o]m[ini] (Latin, meaning: *in the year of our Lord*) 1664

Certificate 3

This is to Satfie to home this may
Consarne that Hanray Miles of
Neuport is A werrey pore man
and not Abell to pay tha harst money
witnest our handes this prasent 6 day
of June 1664
Thomas Champion carche warden
Robart Post Colecter Matt: Goldsmith minist[er]

These three certificates are examples of some of the range of hands that might be in use in a provincial town in the mid-seventeenth century.

The erratic spelling and failure to follow the standard form for these certificates do not appear to have concerned the officials who countersigned them and it is worth noting that none of the witnesses wrote the texts.

Note:
Certificate 3, line 2, the word 'of' is written over another word that has been erased.
Certificate 3, line 4, the transcription 'harst' might be read as 'harſt', 'harst' has been selected by comparison with 'witnest' on the following line.

Scawpwicke

Mr Kollick Clerk — ij
Wm Allen — iiij
Mr David ffoggaty — iiij
Mr Arthur Langworth — ij
Thomas Marre — j
Tho: Craven — ij
Hen: Swanne — ij
John Kirton — ij
Richard Cole — ij
Mrs Mary Dawson — iij
John Hixon — j
Tho Watson — j
John Smyth — j
Wm Swanne — j
John Rydall — j
Robert Marre — j
Robert Swanne — j
Nicholas Kirke — j
Mr Geo: Chippingdale — iij
Jo Richardson — j
Wid Hutchinson — ij
Richard Cole — iij
Richard Cappe — j
John Cooke — j
Robt Pickworth — j
Hugh Reames — ij
David Gash wth a forge — ij
John Rorry — j
Robert Badge — j
Tho: ffisher — j
Richard Clay — j
Rich: Udale — j
Adam Mapleston — j
Wid Rome — j
Abran: Thompson — j

Hearth Tax assessment for Scopwick, Lincolnshire, 1671

Scawpwicke		
Mr Rollick Clerk	ij	
W[illia]m Allen	iiij	
Mr David Foggaty	iiij	
Mr Arthur Langworth	ij	
Thomas Marre	j	
Thomas Crowen	ij	
Hen[ry] Swanne	ij	
John Kirton	ij	
Richard Cole	ij	
Mrs Mary Dawson	iij	
John Hixon	j	
Tho[mas] Watson	j	
John Smyth	j	
W[illia]m Swanne	j	
John Rydalt	j	
Robert Marre		j
Robert Swanne	j	
Nicholas Kirke	j	
Mr Geo[rge] Chippingdale	iij	
Jo Richardson	ij	
Wid[ow] Hutchinson	ij	
Richard Cole	iij	
Richard Cappe	j	
John Cocke	j	
Rob[er]t Pickworth	j	
Hugh Toames	ij	
David Gash w[i]th a forge	ij	
John Torry	j	
Robert Badge	j	
Tho[mas] Fisher	j	
Richard Clay	j	
Rich[ard] Udale	j	
Adam Mapleston	j	
Wid[ow] Toine		j
Fran[cis] Thompson	j	

This Lincolnshire Hearth Tax document, dated 25 April 1671, lists heads of household in the first column, with the number of hearths chargeable for the tax in the second column and the number of exempt heaths in the third.

The first name, Mr Rollick, is followed by his occupation 'clerk', a term commonly used for vicars, rectors or curates, but the scribe has not formed the final letter 'k'.

Several words are abbreviated and may be expanded: Thomas, Richard, William, Robert and widow are all unambiguous, but Jo Richardson may be a Joseph or a John.

The first occurrence of the surname Swanne has a poorly formed final 'e', but the name may be compared with two appearances later in the list.

There are good examples of many capital letters, particularly the long 'C' extending below the line, double 'ff' for 'F' and several curved 'T's. Elsewhere the 'x' in Hixon is typical of this and earlier hands, as are the double 'pp' in Chippingdale, and the single central cross stroke in the 'c' of 'Rollick', 'Cocke', 'Pickworth' and 'Richard'.

Final Concord, Broadwey, Upwey and Nottington, Dorset, 1653

This is the finall Agreem[en]^{t} made in the Court of the Com[m]on Bench at Westm[inste]^{r} from Easter day in fifteene dayes in the yeare of oure
Lord one thousand six hundred fifty three Before Oliver St John John Puliston Peter Warburton & Edward Atkyns Justices &
others then & there p[re]sent Between Sarah Gould Widdow pl[ain]t[iff] and Edward Hyde Esq[uire] & Etheldread his wife & John Winter
Esq[uire] & Frances his wife deforceants of one messuage one garden one orchard fifty & two acres of land fifty acres of meadow eighty #
acres of pasture one acre of wood seaventy acres of furze & heath Com[m]on of pasture for all $^{\&\ all}$ manner of Cattell free fishing goods &
Chattells of felons fugitives felons of them selves & put in the exigend waifes estrayes escheates & deodands w[i]th the appurtenances in
Broadway Upway & Nottington Whereupon a plea of Covenant was sum[m]oned betweene them in the said Court That is to say that
the aforesaid Edward & Etheldread & John & Frances have acknowledged the aforesaid tenem[en]^{ts} Com[m]on of pasture fishing goods & Chattells
of felons fugitives felons of them selves and put in the exigend waifes estrayes escheats & deodands w[i]th the appurtenances to be the right of
her the said Sarah As those w[hi]^{ch} the said Sarah hath of the gift of the aforesaid Edward & Etheldread & John & Frances And those they have ##
remised & quiteclaimed from them the said Edward & Etheldread & John & Frances & their heires to the aforesaid Sarah & her heires for ever
And moreover the said Edward & Etheldread have granted for them & the heires of the said Edward that they will warrant to the aforesaid
Sarah & her heires the aforesaid tenem[en]^{ts} Com[m]on of pasture fishing goods & Chattells of felons fugitives felons of themselves & put in the
exigend waifes & estreyes escheats & deodands w[i]th the appurtenances against them the said Edward & Etheldread & their heires And against the
heires of William Gerard Esq[uire] & Thomas Gerard Esq[uire] for ever And further the said John & Frances have granted for them and the heires of
the said John ## that they will warrant to the aforesaid Sarah & her heires the aforesaid tenem[en]^{t} Com[m]on of pasture fishing goods and Chattells
of felons fugitives felons of them selves & put in the exigend waifes estreyes escheates & deodands w[i]th the appurtenances against them the
heires of William Gerard Esq[uire] & Thomas Gerard Esq[uire] for ever And further the said John and Frances have granted for them and their
heires of
the said John ## that they will warrant to the aforesaid Sarah and her heires the aforesaid tenem[en]^{ts} Com[m]on of pasture fishing goods and
Chattels
of felons fugitives felons of themselves & put in the exigend waifes estreyes estheates & deodands w[i]th the appurenances against them the said John
& Frances & their heires And against the heires of the aforesaid William & Thomas for ever And for this Acknowledgm[en]^{t} remise quiteclaime
warranties fine & Agreem[en]^{t} the same Sarah hath given to the aforesaid Edward and Etheldread & John & Frances two hundred pounds sterlinge

---

This is one of the most difficult hands in this guide, despite others being much older. It is a Court hand which is deliberately archaic, consciously mimicking medieval hands and learnt by the scribe as part of their apprenticeship.

There are many unfamiliar legal terms, but the repetition of standard phrases means that there are several opportunities to examine the same letters and words in a different section where they may be more clearly formed, or there is no interference from letters on the lines above and below.

Note meaningless characters inserted to prevent words being added to this legal document, here represented by the character #.

Herroicke Ladie

Jm the aspect of thie Vnparraled Bewtie and
rare Virtues I am Powerfullie overcome.
Thine eiyes which are more Cleare then bright
ayre more dazlinge then Sunn Beames
and Percinge as an Instrument of death
haue made soe deepe an Inscition in my
Breest; that I am fforced to implore yor
ffauor apprehendinge noe healinge medicine in any
butt thie sealfe) to fforme mee in thie
loue. Judging thatt to bee my Transcendant
Happines and cause of my greatest joy
and Triumph. thatt I maie Remaine

Alcester the 5 of July: 1621

Yor most humble Servitur
in any office you Commaunde
mee. ffulke Madeley.

Love letter from Fulke Madeley of Alchester, Oxfordshire, 1652

Reproduced by permission of the More Molyneux Family

Heroicke Ladie

Inn the aspect of thie unparraled Bewtie and
rare virtues I am Powerffullie overcome
Thine eyes which are more cleare then brigh[t]
ayre more dazlinge then sunn Beames
and Percinge as an Instrument of death
have made soe deepe an Inscition in my
Brest thatt I am Forced t^o implore yo^ur
Favo^ur (apprehendinge noe healing ^medicine in any
butt thie sealfe) to Itermize mee in thie
love judging thatt to bee my Transcendant
Happines and cause of my greatest joy
and Triumph thatt I may Remaine

Alcester the 5th	Yo^ur most humble seruitur
of July 1652	in any office you Commande
	mee Fulke Madeley

Fulke Madeley's heartwarming love letter to his unnamed heroic lady is in a quite standard Italic hand, made much more difficult by his unconventional spelling and a few awkward letters. Many documents have not been kept in ideal conditions for three or four hundred years and water, mould, insects and rodents are not the friends of paper and parchment. Some of the problems encountered in interpreting these documents derive from the folds, holes, tears and smudges that they have acquired.

Throughout this text the small letter 'p' may be difficult to recognise. In *deepe, implore* and *apprehendinge* (lines 6, 7 and 8) the 'p' is much more like the familiar form of a long 's' dropping below the line followed by a short 's' which might be expected in seventeenth century Italic hands.

The initial 'u' and 'v' in *unparraled* and *virtues* (lines 2 and 3) will be familiar to those with some experience of Secretary hands, as will the abbreviations at the end of *your* and *favour* (lines 8 and 9).

Quarter booke of all the Entryes both Inwards & Outwards, in the porte of Maldon for the qrter ending upon ye 24th daye of June Anno Dni 1649.

Inwards

9o Aprilis 1649

Out of ye providence of London Michaell Yokley Mr from Amsterdam. Hans Corneliis Smirobeck al. ffower hundred Beaver wombes & six yards of Scarlett cloath of ffrance — — —	Subs —02: 11: 04 15 p Ct—00: 07: 08½ Subs neat 02: 03: 07½ Custom—00: 12: 10 02: 16: 05½
eodem die Out of ye providence of London Mich. Yokley Mr from Amsterdam. Tobias Gurnet ind. twenty pounds of Rubarb ffortye pounds of Mace & halfe a hundred wght. of Latin wyer.	Subs —03: 03: 04 15 p Ct—00: 09: 06 Subs neat 02: 13: 10
vto Maij 1649 Out of a wreckd shipp cast away at ye East Swale John Mathewes ind. ffive thousand of Orringes — — — — —	Subs —00: 05: 00 15 p Ct—00: 00: 09 Subs neat 00: 04: 03
Summ total	05: 14: 06½ ob

Outwards

Entryes — — — — — Null.

Jo. Lukyn Coll.

Customs Book from Maldon, Essex, 1649

Quarter book of all the Entryes both Inward[es] & Outward[es]
in the Porte of Maldon for the q[uar]ter ending upon the
24th daye of June *Anno D[omi]ni* [Latin meaning: *in the year of our Lord*] 1649

Inward[es]

ij^{o} Apri[il]is [*secundo Aprilis*, Latin meaning: *the second of April*] 1649

Out of the providence of London Michaell Yokeley	}	subs[idy]	02:11:04
M[aste]r from Amsterdam	}	15 p[er] C	00:07:08½
Hans Cornelius Lincobeck al[ien] Fower hundred -	}	Subs[idy] neat	02:03:07½
Beaver wombes & six yard[es] of Scarlet cloath	}	Customs	00:12:10
of France		[Total]	02:16:05½

eodem die [Latin meaning: *the same day*]

Out of the Providence of London Mich[aell] Yokeley	}	Subs[idy]	03:03:04
M[aste]r from Amsterdam	}	15 p[er] C	00:09:06
Tobias Gurnet ind[igenous] Twentye pound[es] of Rubarb	}		
Fortye pound[es] of Mace & halfe a hundred	}	Subs[idy] neat	02:13:01
w[eig]ht of Latin Wyer	}		

v^{to} Maij [*Quinto Maij*, Latin meaning: *the fifth of May*] 1649

Out of a wreked shipp East away at the East swale	}	Subs[idy]	00:05:00
John Mathewes ind[igenous] Five thousand of	}	15 p[er] C	00:00:09
Oringes	}		
		Subs[idy] neat	00:04:03
		Sum total	05:14:06½

Outward[es]

Entryes — *Null[us]* [Latin: *nothing*]

Jo: Lukyn, Coll[ector]

Note:
Occasional use of Latin was common in seventeenth century documents. *Anno Domini* is usually translated 'in the year of our Lord', rather than 'in the year of the Lord'.

The Roman numeral 'C' (100) is used on lines 7 and 13 for the collector's cut of the subsidy, 15 parts per hundred or 15 per cent.

Beaver wombes, line 9, are the softer, more valuable, beaver hide from the belly of the animal.

Many official records use technical terms that would have been immediately recognised by the intended reader, but are not always obvious today. Here al[ien] and ind[igenous] merchants paid different rates of duty on their imports so the clerks and collectors always noted their status.

Kalender del domo Correccois

Rose Lane – To remaine in the house of Correction untill next Sessions and the discretions of the Justice of Lyme Interim ita to provide her necessary clothes to weare in meane tyme

Grace Symmys – To remaine in the house of Correction for a whole yeare from the tyme of her Committment.

John Dent – To remaine in the house of Correction untill next Sessions.

Elinotha Dunters – discharged, and ordered to get a Mr wthin a Monthe els to be sent backe to the house of Correction.

Nathaniell Saunders – discharged uppon tryall.

Christian Slade – discharged.

Ralph Hamwaye – To remaine in the house of Correction untill he be discharged by Roger Colley Esqr.

George Wootton and Christian Evans – To be well whipt and delivered and sent by passe from tythinge to tythinge (beinge very dangerous persons) unto the Cittye of Exon.

Dorset Quarter Sessions, Calendar of the House of Correction, 1629

Kalender del domo Correcc[ti]o[n]is [Latin meaning: *Calendar of the House of Correction*]

Rose Lane	{ To remaine in the house of Correcc[ti]on untill next { Sessions and the p[ar]ishioners of the p[ar]ish of Ryme { Intrincica to p[ro]vide her necessary cloathes to weare in { meane tyme
Grace Spinny	{ To remaine in the house of Correcc[ti]on for a whole { yeare from the tyme of her Committm[en]^{t}
John Bent	To remaine in the house of Correcc[ti]on until next Sessions.
Gilmotha Curters	{ Discharged and ordered to get a m[aste]^{r} w[i]thin a moneth { els to be sent backe to the house of Correcc[ti]on.
Othaniell Saunders	{ Discharged uppon tryall.
Christian Slade	{ Discharged.
Ralph Samwayes	{ To remaine in the house of Correcc[ti]on untill { he be discharged by Roger Gollop Esq[ui]^{r}[e].
George Wootton and Christian Seamo[ur]	{ To be well whipt and deliv[er]ed and sent by passe { from Tythinge to Tythinge (beinge very dange { rous p[er]sons) unto the Cittye of Exon[ia] [the Latin form of *Exeter*].

This short document, in a typical Secretary hand, contains many challenging elements.

The first line is in Latin: opening sentences or introductory titles were often written in Latin a means of validating certain legal documents. This should not deter the researcher and is easily overcome.

Throughout the text the scribe has a curious affectation of extending the letter 'f' at the end of words in a flourish like a superscript 'e'.

Line 3 has the standard 'par' abbreviation in *parishioners* and *parish* which may be contrasted with the 'pro' abbreviation on the following line in *provide.*

The terminal 'e' has an open form in *Ryme, Rose* and *meane,* but a closed form in *Lane, weare* and *tyme,* lines 4-5.

The capitals 'G' and 'S' have similar forms. It is useful that they appear in the unambiguous and familiar forename *Grace* and the subject of the text *Sessions,* as the 'G' next appears in the uncommon forename *Gilmotha,* lines 3, 6, 8 and 9.

This text also contains the unusual male forename Othaniell. Generally, there is a wider variety of female forenames in Tudor and Stuart texts, although many seventeenth century men were given obscure biblical names.

Thornhill — Mrs Barbar Thornhill in annuities — xls
George Thornhill Esq in landes — xvj li
Robert Hill in goodes — iiij li
Robert Boulsbury a recusant in Coppie — viij li
John Gaydon by coppie — xx s
John Lamme in coppie — xx s
George Corbett in coppie — xx s
Willm Rock Clerk in coppie — xx s
Robert Lambe in coppie — xx s
Willm Mariott in coppie — xx s

Stowslay — John Willoughby in landes — xls
Anne Frank Wid in Coppie — vj li
Willm Sidlin in goodes — vj li
Willm Cowlett in Coppie — xls
Thomas Cox in Coppie — xx s

Caundle wake — Joan Burt in landes — xls
Robert Knight in landes — xx s
George Membridge in coppie — xx s
Margery Appling by lease — xx s
Thomas Horne in goodes — viij li

Starton Caundle — Elizabeth Hoppe Wid in coppie — vj li
Gilles Bartlett in goodes — iiij li
Joane Aplin in Coppies — xx s
James Coder in Coppies — xx s
Thomas Gilbitt in coppie — xx s

Dorset Lay Subsidy Return, 1628

Thornehill	Mr Barbar Thornehill in Annuitie	xl^{s}
	George Thornehill Esq[uire] in land[es]	viij^{li}
	Robert Hill in good[es]	iiij^{li}
	Robert Goulsbury a recusant in Coppie	viij^{li}
	John Capen by coppie	xx^{s}
	John Sanne in coppie	xx^{s}
	George Lockett in coppie	xx^{s}
	Will[ia]m Rocke Clerk in coppie	xx^{s}
	Robert Coombe in coppie	xx^{s}
	Will[ia]m Paviott in coppie	xx^{s}
Gom[er]shay	John Willingsby in land	xl^{s}
	Anne Jeanes wid[ow] in Copie	iij^{li}
	Will[ia]m Gidlin in Good[es]	iij^{li}
	Will[ia]m Hewlett in Coppie	xl^{s}
	Thomas Hix in Coppie	xx^{s}
Candle Wake	John Burt in land	xl^{s}
	Robert King in Land[es]	xx^{s}
	George Allembridg in coppie	xx^{s}
	Margery Appling by lease	xx^{s}
	Thomas Thorne in good[es]	viij^{li}
Starton }	Elizabeth Pope Wid[ow] in coppie	iij^{li}
Candle }	Gilles Bartlett in good[es]	iij^{li}
	Joane Aplin in Coppie	xx^{s}
	James Loder in Coppie	xx^{s}
	Thomas Gilbitt in coppie	xx^{s}

This document contains many capital letters and is a good introduction to Secretary hand. The repetition of goods, lands, coppie (copyhold) provides an opportunity to build confidence and check accuracy.

Dalham 1612

A Terrier of the Glebe-Lande and
howses belonginge to the Rectorye or
Parsonage of dalham dated the thyrd daye
of Januarye Ao 1612.

1 Inprimis one mansion or dwellynge house one
backhouse & barne, houses for necessary uses
one orchard & one gardine
Item one barne one stable & one Close of
pasture conteyninge by estimation one acer
more adioyninge to the sayed barne & stable.
Item one pece of meadowe laye grounde and
2 arable lyenge together nere unto moulton
conteyninge by estimation three acres.
the meadowe lieth betwene the meadowe of
George Drurye gent. & conteyneth by estimation
a acre the one syde abutteth upon the broke
towarde the weste & the one end abutteth
upon the meadowe of the forsayd George Drurye
towarde the East & the other ende upon the sayd
broke towarde ~~the~~ moulton & towarde the north
& the arable land abutteth upon the landes
of dyvers men towarde the East & the
one end abutteth upon the foresayd broke towarde
the north & the other end towarde the East.

Glebe terrier of Dalham, Suffolk, 1613

Dalha[m] 1613
A Terriar of the Glebe Land[es] and
howses belonginge to the Rectorye or
p[ar]sonage of dalha[m] dated the thyrd daye
of Januarye A[nn]o [Latin meaning: *the year*] 1613
Inprimis [Latin meaning: *Firstly*] one mansion or dwellinge howse one
backhowse & two, howses for necessary uses
one orchard & one gardine ————
It[e]m one barne one stable & one Close of
pasture Contayninge by estimation one Acer
nere adjoynynge to the sayd barne & stable /
It[e]m one pece of medowe Laye ground and
Arable Lyenge together nere unto moulton
Contayninge by estimation Six acres /
the medowe lieth at bothe end[es] of the medowe of
George Traycye gent[leman] & Co[n]tayneth by estimation
v Rodes the one seyde abuttethe upon the broke
toward[es] the weste & the one end abutteth
upon the medow of the forsayd Gorge Traycie
toward[es] the Easte & the other ende upone the sayd
broke toward[es] ~~the~~ moulton & toward[es] the north
& the Arable land abutteth upon the Landes
of dyvers menes toward[es] the East & the
one end abutt[es] upon the forsayd broke toward[es]
the north & the other end toward[es] the East.

This is a somewhat untidy Secretary hand with some crossing-out and insertions, which add to the confusion. It is often difficult to distinguish between capital and small letters, particularly 'A' and 'D'. Horizontal and forward slash strokes at the end of lines fill the space to prevent later insertion and are common in legal documents of this period.

Inprimis (Latin for 'firstly') and Item (Latin for 'likewise') are commonly used to signify first and subsequent entries in a list.

The general abbreviation stroke of a horizontal line over a word is used here in Dalha[m] (lines 1 and 4), It[e]m (lines 9 and 12) and co[n]tayneth (line 16).

This scribe has used the same symbol to indicate the abbreviation of 'par' in p[ar]sonage (line 4) and 'pri' in Inp[ri]mis (line 6). A tutor f the period might mark this as 'technically incorrect' as separate symbols were used for these abbreviations by most scribes.

Note: the poorly formed shoulderless 'h' at the end of 'north' (line 21) which resembles the contraction for 'es' at the end of words throughout the text.

Calne Borough

177 Certayne disorders committed in the Boroughe of Calne, and presented to be reformed at the Quarter Sessions holden at the Devizes the [illegible] of Aprill 1612.

Imprimis we present Gyles Colliar of Calne for sellinge of Ale contrarie to the statute not beinge thereunto licensed and for keepinge of unlawfull companie in his howse at unlawfull seasons and tymes.

Item we present Phillipp Edwardes and Edward Carine and John Coate thinckers for resortinge to the same howse at unlawfull howers of the night.

Item we present Edwarde Masie for sellinge of Ale without licence and for baytinge of his Bulle uppon holie daies contrarie to the kinges Majesties Injunctions and will also be drunke.

Item we present John Grosse Tipler because he will be [illegible] himselfe, and Lucretia his wife, because she is a woman of corrupt communication, and therefore they are unfit to keepe an Ale house, in regard whereof we desire to have them discharged, and because they have not sufficient beddinge to lodge poore travellers when neede shall be.

Item we present William Basse Tipler, because he interteyneth mens servants at his howse when they shoulde be in theyr Masters howse, and his wife is a woman that scorneth religion, for when she is requested to goe to the churche, she answereth that she must tarrie at home to keepe the pott, least peradventure her porridge shoulde runne over; and besides that they have no bedd to lodge any passingers, and he is a Carpenter by crafte, and is able to live without Ale keepinge and therefore we desyre that they maye be forbidden to sell ale any more.

Item we present Humphrie Bisshope for sellinge ale without any lycense.

Item we desyre to have the number of Alehowses to be diminished in the Towne of Calne for they doe all brewe the strongest Ale and thither do resorte all the great drunkers both of the Towne and Countrie to spende theyr tyme in idlenes and theyr monie in excessive drinkinge, and beinge partly drunke and halfe mad, no officer can well iudge whether they be drunke yea or no, and therefore can not punishe them according to the Lawe, and all men for the most part love these cupp companions so well, that no man will take uppon him to be a sworne witnes against any drunkard. It were greatly to be wisshed that all Alesellers might be compelled to make theyr Ale a great deale smaller and to sell a full Quart for a penny, otherwise this synne of drunkennes will never be avoyded, men are so bewitched with the sweetenes of stronge lycour.

John Moore
John Rillinge Constables.
his + marke. X

Presentment of the Constables of Calne borough to the Quarter Sessions, Devizes, Wiltshire, 1612

Calne Borough

Certayne disorders committed in the Boroughe of Calne, and presented to be reformed at the Quarter Sessions holden at the Devizes the xxj[th] of Aprill 1612.

Inprimis we present Gyles Helliar of Calne for sellinge of Ale contrarie to the statute not beinge thereunto licensed [and] and for kepinge of unlawfull companie in his howse at unlawfull seasons, and tymes.
Item we present Phillipe Edwardes and Edward Gawine and John Coate thunger for resortinge to the same howse at unlawfull howers of the night.

Item we present Edwarde Masie for sellinge of Ale w[i][th]out License and for baytinges of his Bulle uppon Holie daies contrarie to the Kinges Ma[jes]ties Iniunctions and [he] will also be drunke

Item we present John Scotte Tipler because he will be tipmirrie himselfe, and Lucretia his wife, because she is a wooma[n] of corrupt comunication, and therefore they are unfit to kepe and Ale house, in regard whereof we desyre to have them discarded, and because they have not sufficient beddinge to lodge poore travelers when neede shall be.

Item we present William Bushe Tipler, because he intertayneth mens servants at his howse when they shoulde be in theyer Masters howse, and his wife is a woman that skorneth relligion, for when she is requested to goe to the churche, she aunswereth that she must tarrie at home to Keele the potte, least p[er]adventure her porridge shoulde rune over, and besides that they have ~~but one~~ no bedd to lodge any passingers and he is a Carpenter by crafte, and is able to live w[i][th]out Ale Keepinge and therefore we desyre that they maye be forbidden to sell ale any more.

Item, we present Humphrie Bishope for selling ale w[i][th]out any lycense.

Item we desyre to have the nomber of Alehowses to be diminished in the Towne of Calne for they doe all brewe a vie who maye brewe the strongest Ale and thither do resorte all the great drinkers bothe of the Towne and Countrie to spende theyer tyme in idlenes and theyer monie in excessivie drinkinge, and beinge partly drunke and halfe mad, no officer can well judge whether they be drunke yea or no, and therefore can not punishe [them] according to the Lawe, and all me[n] for the most p[ar]te love these cupp companions so well, that no man will take uppon him to be a sworne witnes against any drunkard.
It were greatly to be wisshed that all Ale sellers might be compelled to make theyer Ale a great deale smaller and to sell a full Quart for a pennie, otherwise this sinne of drunkennes will never be avoyded men are so bewitched w[i][th] the sweetenes of stronge Lycoure
John Noyes, John Killinge, Constables
his + marke X

A typical neat Secretary hand of the early seventeenth century. Note the long 's' and shoulderless 'h' dropping below the line. The different hand shows that John Killinge alone signed his name, while John Noyes added his mark.

Sr when Mr Doctor Wilkinson beinge wth you at Edington I
moued you in the behalfe of a poore woman one Elizabeth
Carpenter who hath donne amisse wth a man of myne
this bearer James Wade, and you promised me to doe
them bothe all the lawfull favoure you might, sithence
wch tyme, one Cod hath warned bothe of them to
appeare at Salisbury on Satterday next, And althoughe
they be poore yet very unwillinge to undergoe an
open disgrace, in regard the one is my man &
the other was my sisters servant, And to their
wellwishers aswell they shall shew themselves thankfull
for the kyndnes you shall doe them therin, as I my
selfe in their behalfe and what favoure you can
doe them touchinge my request I doe desire ~~you~~
to knowe by this bearer, And so wth my kinde
[illegible] to you I wyl end

Yor assured frend.

Henry Longe

Letter of Juell Longe to the official of the bishop of Salisbury, undated, probably 1612

Good m[aster] Doctor Wilkinson beinge w[i]th you at Edington I
moved you in the behalfe of a poore woman one Elizabeth
Paynter, whoe hath donne amisse w[i]th a man of myne
this bearer James Reade, and you p[ro]missed me to doe
the bothe all the lawfull favoure you might, Sithence
w[hi]^{ch} tyme, one Tod hath warned bothe of them to
appeare at Salisbury on satterday next, And although
they be poore yet very unwillinge to receave an
open disgrace, in regard the one is my man &
the other was my sisters servant, and to theyr
powers aswell they shall shew themselves thankfull
for the kyndnes you shall doe them herin, as I my
selfe in theyr behalfe and what favoure you can
doe them toutchinge my request I doe desire ~~you~~
to knowe by this bearer And so w[i]th my kinde
love to you I rest ev[er]
Yo[u]r assured frend
Juell Longe

This is a typical secretary hand.

Note the contractions of w[i]th in which the shoulderless 'h' drops below the line (lines 1 and 3).

The right leg of the capital 'R' kicking the following letter in *Reade* (line 4), similarly the right leg of 'k' in *kindnes* (line 12).

A good example of the interchangeable small letters 'u' and 'v' is found in *very unwilling* (line 8).

The standard abbreviation stroke for 'er' may be difficult to interpret in short words such as *ever* (line 16).

The xxith day of June Edmund Pilman of
purton and Agnes Hambledon were maried

Ao Dom The xth day of July William Turky and Elizabeth
1599 Tamison were maried.

The xxvth day of February Nicholas Tibor of
Berwik and Anne weller of Marlborough were maried

Ao Dom The xvth day of May John Albery and Elizabeth
1600 Smith were maried.

The xxxith day of June Richard Spire and Margery
Lewe of ye pish of Brightwell in the county of Bark
were maried.

The xxvith day of October John Hodson and
Mary ford were maried.

Ao Dom The xxvth of July Richard Spiar and Agnes
1603 Broughton of Bonsington were maried.

Ao Dom The xiijth day of October Robert Rosse and
1604 Anne Wookes were maried.

The vth day of November Joyce Lane and
John More were maried.

Ao Dom The xxith day of July Thomas cleere and
1605 Joane Smith of the pish of Sherburne were maried

The xxith day of September Edmund Flecher
and Elizabeth Hargrove were maried

The xxith day of October Robert Smith and
Johane Wisse of Drayton were maried

Brightwell Baldwin, Oxfordshire, parish register, 1598-1605

	The xjth dey of June Edmund Gilman of
	purton and Agnis Hambledon were maried
A[nn]o Do[mi]ni	The xth dey of July William Tucky and Elizabeth
1599	Tainnison were maried.
	The xxvth dey of February Nicholas Gibes of
	Berwik and Anne weller of Warbrough were maried
A[nn]o Do[mi]ni	The xvth dey of May John Albery and Elizabeth
1600	Smith were maried.
	The xxxth dey of June Richard Spire and Margery
	Lever of p[ar]ish of Brightwell in the county of Bark
	were maried.
	The xxvjth dey of October John Hodson and
	Mary Ford were maried.
A[nn]o Do[mi]ni	The xth of July Richard Spiar and Agnis
1603	Broughton of Bensington were maried.
A[nn]o Do[mi]ni	The xiiijth dey of October Robert Rosse and
1604	Anne Weekes were maried.
	The xth dey of November Joyce Lane and
	John New were maried.
A[nn]o Do[mi]ni	The xxijth dey of July Thomas cleere and
1605	Joane Smith of the p[ar]ish of Shurburne were maried.
	The xxjth dey of September Edmund Flecher
	and Elizabeth Hargrove weere maried.
	The xxijth dey of October Robert Smith and
	Johane Wisse of Drayton were maried.

A typical secretary hand from the turn of the seventeenth century.

Note:
The scribe does not always use capitals for proper nouns: *weller* and *Warbrough* (line 6). The double 'F' for a capital is usual, *February* (line 5), but a large single 'F' in *Ford* (line 13) is clearly intended to be a capital.

Small 'h' has almost entirely lost its shoulder throughout the text.

The surname *Tainnison* (line 4) is particularly difficult as there is nothing to distinguish the series of minims which might be the letters 'i', 'm', 'n' or 'u'. Fortunately the two 'i's are dotted, but this is not always the case in this text, or with other scribes, for instance: *Elizabeth* (line 3) and *Berwik* (line 6).

The use of the Julian calendar discussed in the dating section of the introduction.

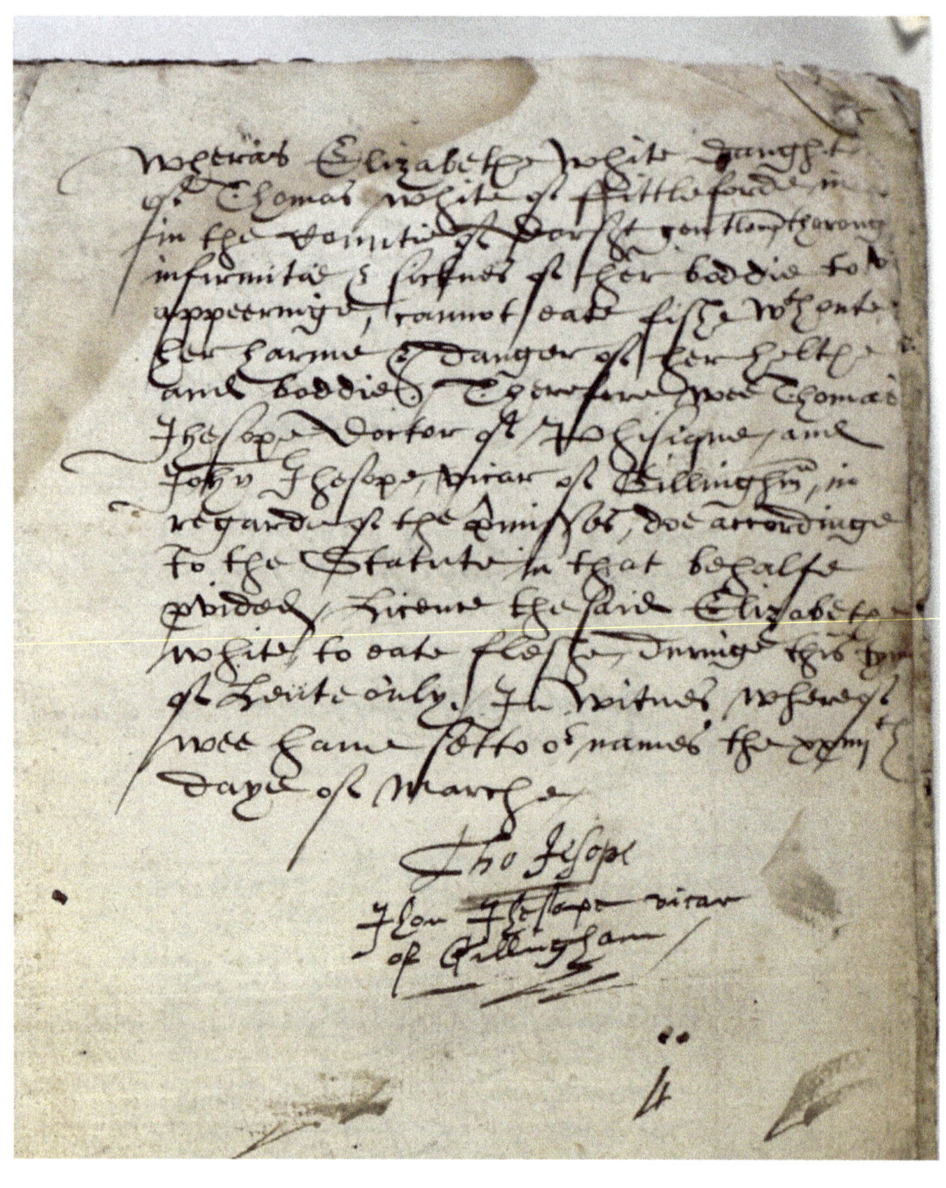

Whereas Elizabeth White daughter
of Thomas White of ffittleforde in
in the Countie of Dorset gentleman throughe
infirmities & sicknes of her boddie to hir
appertaininge, cannot eate fishe without
her harme & danger of her helth
and boddie, Therefore wee Thomas
Jessope Doctor of Phisique and
John Jessope vicar of Gillingham, in
regarde of the premisses, doe accordinge
to the Statute in that behalfe
provided, licence the said Elizabeth
White, to eate fleshe duringe this time
of Lente only. In witnes whereof
wee have sette or names the xxvj[th]
daye of Marche.

Tho Jessope

John Jessope vicar
of Gillingham

Licence for a Gillingham, Dorset, parishioner to eat meat during Lent, 1595

Whereas Elizabethe White Daught[er]
of Thomas White of Fittleforde in[n]
in the Countie of Dors[e]t gentlema[n] thoroug[h]
infirmitie & sicknes of her boddie to u[s]
appeeringe, cannot eate fishe w[i]^th^oute
her harme & danger of her helthe
and boddie. Therefore wee thomas
Jhesope Doctor of Phisique, and
John Jhesope, vicar of Gillingh[a]m, in
regarde of the p[re]misses, doe accordinge
to the Statute in that behalfe
p[ro]vided, licence the said Elizabethe
White to eate fleshe duringe this tym[e]
of Lente only. In Witnes whereof
wee have set to o[ur] names the xxiiij^th^
daye of marche
Tho Jesope
Jhon Jhesope vicar
of Gillingham

This is a typical Secretary hand of the late sixteenth century with additional difficulties caused by the loss of some text in the right margin and the interference of descenders in the following lines.

Note:

The kicking 'k' of 'sickness' (line 4) crossed through by the descender from 'of' (line 3).

The shoulderless 'h' throughout, but particularly difficult when dropping down in the abbreviated 'w[i]^th^oute' (line 5).

The almost horizontal backward leaning ascenders of 'danger' (line 6), 'regarde' and 'accordinge' (line 10) and 'daye' (line 16).

The similar capitals 'E' in 'Elizabeth' (line 1) and 'G' in 'Gillingham' (line 9).

The 'ur' abbreviation in o[ur] (line 15).

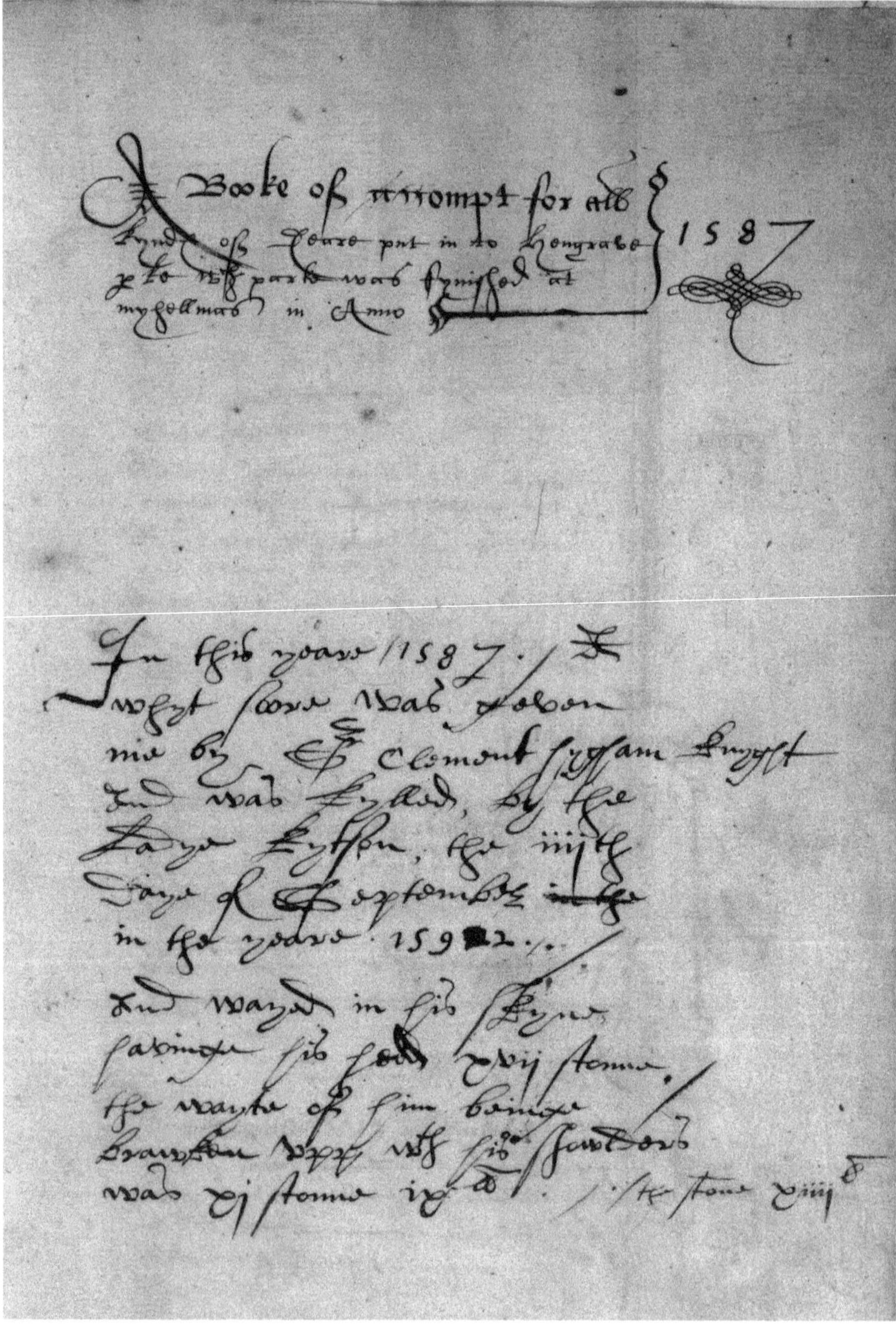

The Booke of accompt for all
kinde of Deare put in to Hengrave
parke which parke was fynished at
mydsomer in Anno 1587

In this yeare 1587. / The
whyt soore was stolen
me by Sir Clement Higham knight
and was kylled, by the
Ladye Kytson, the iiijth
daye of September in the
in the yeare 1592./.
And wayed in his skyne
havinge his hed xvij stone,
the wayte of him beinge
brawned xxij with his shoulders
was xj stone ix li. / the stone viij li

Account Book of Hengrave Park, Suffolk, 1587

A Book of accompt for all[e] }
kynd[es] of Deare put in to Hengrave }
p[ar]ke w[hi]^{ch} parke was fynished at } 1587
myhellmas (*sic.*) in Anno [Latin meaning: *the year*] }

In this yeare / 1587 / A
whyt soore was geven
me by S[i]^{r} Clement hygham knyght
and was kylled, by the
Ladye Kytson, the iiijth
Daye of September ~~in the~~
in the yeare 1592.
And wayed in his skyne
savinge his hedd xvij stonne,
the wayte of him beinge
brawken upp w[i]th his showlders
was xj stonne ix^{ll} /the ston[n]e xiiij$^{l[bs]}$

An irregular hand, but distinguished by the writer's efforts to make a visual display with the addition of a decorative capital 'A' at the start and a typically sixteenth and seventeenth century device of interlocking loops below the date 1587. Impressive capitals are common, but frequently give way to less impressive text!

Note: in words such as 'all[e]' (line 1) the final abbreviation stroke may be genuinely intended to represent the omission of a letter or simply a flourish.

In cases where the spelling or form is particularly odd it may be necessary to insert *sic.* [meaning: *thus*] to indicate the omission of a letter, in this case the 'c' from Michaelmas. It should be used sparingly to indicate that the text does not contain a typographical or transcription error.

The superscript ll on the final line indicates one of the possible abbreviations for the plural of *libra*, a pound. Localised uses for weights and measures meant that at the end of the text it was necessary to specify how many pounds were in a stone.

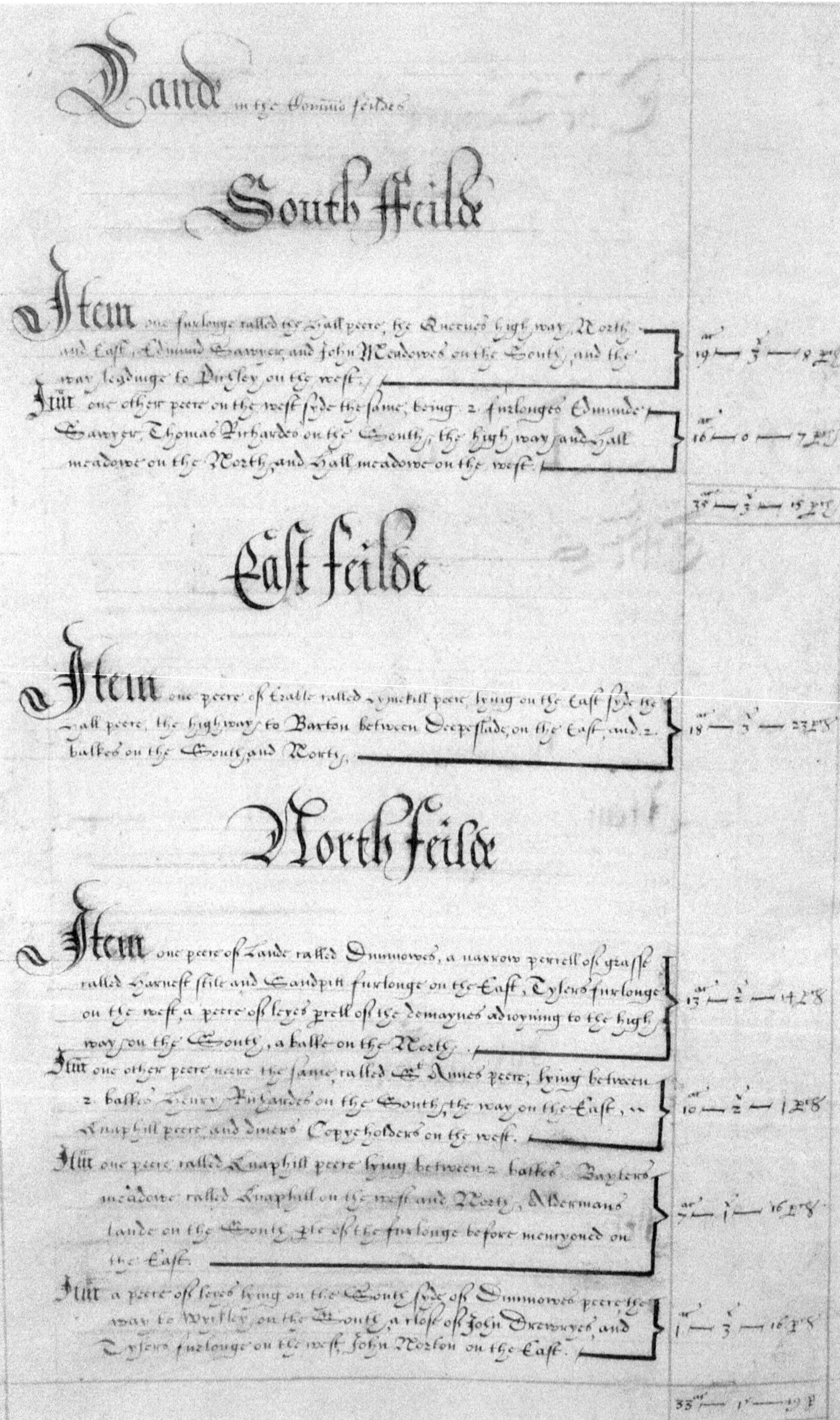

Lande in the Commune feildes

South ffeilde

Item one furlonge called the Hall peece, the Queenes high way North
and East, Edmund Sawyer, and John Meadowes on the South, and the
way leading to Pirley on the west. } 19 ar. — 3 r. — 8 per.

Item one other peece on the west syde the same, being 2 furlonges Edmunde
Sawyer, Thomas Richardes on the South, the high way and Hall
meadowe on the North, and Hall meadowe on the west. } 16 ar. — 0 — 7 per.

35 ar. — 3 r. — 15 per.

East feilde

Item one peece of Erable called Lymekill peece, lying on the East syde the
Hall peece, the highway to Barton between Deepeslade, on the East, and 2
balkes on the South and North. } 18 ar. — 3 r. — 23 per.

North feilde

Item one peece of Lande called Dunmowes, a narrow percell of grasse
called Harnest stile and Sandpitt furlonge on the East, Tysons furlonge
on the west, a peece of leyes prell of the demaynes adioyning to the high
way on the South, a balke on the North. } 13 ar. — 2 r. — 14 per.

Item one other peece neere the same, called St Annes peece, lying between
2 balkes Henry Richardes on the South, the way on the East, &
Knaphill peece and divers Copyholders on the west. } 10 ar. — 2 r. — 1 per.

Item one peece called Knaphill peece lying between 2 balkes Baylers
meadowe called Knaphill on the west and North, Aldermans
lande on the South, ple of the furlonge before mentyoned on
the East. } 7 ar. — 1 r. — 16 per.

Item a peece of leyes lying on the South syde of Dunmowes peece the
way to Writley on the South, a close of John Drewryes, and
Tysons furlonge on the west, John Norton on the East. } 1 ar. — 3 r. — 16 per.

35 ar. — 1 r. — 19 per.

Survey of Kettering, Northamptonshire, by Ralph Treswell, 1585

Lande in the Commo[n] feildes

South Feilde

Item one furlonge called the Hall peece, the Queenes high way, North }
and East, Edmund Sawyer, and John Meadowes on the South, and the }
way leadinge to Pichley on the west }19 ac[res] – 3 r[ods] – 8 p[er]ch[es]

It[e]m one other peece on the west syde the same, being 2 furlonges Edmunde }
Sawyer, Thomas Richardes on the South, the high way and Hall }
meadowe on the North, and Hall meadowe on the west. } 16 ac[res] – 0 r[ods] – 7 p[er]ch[es]

35 ac[res] – 3 r[ods] – 15 p[er]ch[es]

East Feilde

Item one peece of Erable called Lymekill peece on the East syde the }
Hall peece, the highway to Barton between Deepeslade, on the East, and 2 }
balkes on the South and North } 18 ac[res] – 3 r[ods] – 23 p[er]ch[es]

North feilde

Item one peece of Lande called Dunmowes, a narrow percell of grasse }
called Harvest stile and Sandpitt furlonge on the East, Tylers furlonge }
on the west, a peece of leyes p[ar]cell of the demaynes adjoyning to the high }
way on the South, a balke on the North } 13 ac[res] – 2 r[ods] – 14 p[er]ch[es]

It[e]m one other peece neere the same , called S[ain]t Annes peece, lying between }
2 balkes Henry Richardes on the South, the way on the East, # }
Knaphill peece and divers Copyeholders on the west } 10 ac[res] – 2 r[ods] – 1 p[er]ch[es]

It[e]m one peece called Knaphill peece lying between 2 balkes, Baxters }
meadowe called Knaphill on the west and North, Aldermans }
lande on the South p[ar]te of the furlonge before mencyoned on }
the East } 7 ac[res] – 1 r[ods] – 16 p[er]ch[es]

It[e]m a peece of leyes lying on the South syde of Dunmowes peece, the }
way to Wyckley on the South, a close of John Drewryes, and }
Tylers furlonge on the west, John Norton on the East. } 11 ac[res] – 3 r[ods] – 16 p[er]ch[es]

A very clear late sixteenth century Secretary hand from a document compiled for display as well as reference. It was the culmination of several months of surveying and was intended to impress.

Note: there is very little difference, even in size, between capital and small 'h' and the uncommon letters 'j' and 'x' in 'adjoining' and 'Baxters' may be difficult to recognise (lines 16 and 21).

There are good examples of the series of minims forming the letters 'n', 'm', and 'u' in the place name Dunmowes (lines 14 and 25).

In the name of god Amen. I Bastian bond visited wth sicknes
and weak in body doe mak my last will and testament in manner
and forme as here after followeth. first I commit my
soule in to the hands of almighty god & my bodie to be
buried in the church yard of henly. Item I give and
bequeath unto my wife Alce bond every part and pcell
of my goods wholy as yt standeth and remaineth in my dwelling
house excepting, a cloke, a black pare of
venshons, and my best whight canvas dublet, wch I give
unto my brother thomas bonde, & paiinge unto my wife
Alce bond xs of good and lawfull monye. further more
I leve my saide wife Alce bonde to be my full and lawfull
executor to enioy all my goods and to paye all detts
what soe ever shalbe lawfully demanded in this my
last will and testament. to all wch things I willingly consent
in the xxvith yeare of the raigne of our soveran ladie Elizabeth
by the grace of god Queen of england france and
Ireland defendres of the faith. and viij of January
anno domi 1584. in the presence of these whose names ar
under scribed as lawfull wittnesses.

Gregory Grove the [struck through]

The mark of William Stentone.

The mark of + Thomas Tabot.

Will of Bastian Bord, Oxfordshire, 1584

In the name of god Amen. I ~~t~~ Bastian Bord visited w[i]th sicknes
and weak in body doe mak my last will and testament in manner
and forme as heer after followeth. first I commit my
soule in to the hands of almighty god & my bodie to be
buried in the church yeard of henly. Item I gev and
bequeath unto my wif Aels Bord every part and percell
of my goods wholy as yt standeth and remaineth in my dwell[ing]
house ~~w[hi]^{ch} is in the~~ exeptinge a cloke *a blacke paire of*
venesions, and my best whight canvas dublet, w[hi]^{ch} I gev
unto my brother Thomas Borde, he paieinge unto my wif
Aels Bord x^{s} of good and lawfull money. further more
I leve my saide wif Aels Borde to be my full and lawfull
Executor to enjoy all my goods and to $^{\text{reseve and}}$ paie all debts
what soe ever shalbe be lawfully demanded in this my
last will and testament. to all w[hi]^{ch} things I willingly consent
in the xxvijth year of the raine of our soveran ladie Elizabeth
by the grac of god # Quen of England Fraunc and
Iirland defendor[e]s of the faithand the iij Jenuary
Anno do[mi]ni 1584 in the presenc of thes who ar
under scribed as lawfull wittnesses

	Gregory Grove the [~~illegible~~]
The mark of	~~w~~ willia[m] WS Stentone
The makk of T of	Thomas Tabet

An untidy, but typical secretary hand of the later sixteenth century. The copy of this will in the diocesan register is much clearer: for instance *reseve*, interlineate line 13, is entered in the copied text as *receyve*. However, in the tidy diocesan copy several useful features are missing, such as the differentiation between those witnesses who could sign their names and those who left their marks.

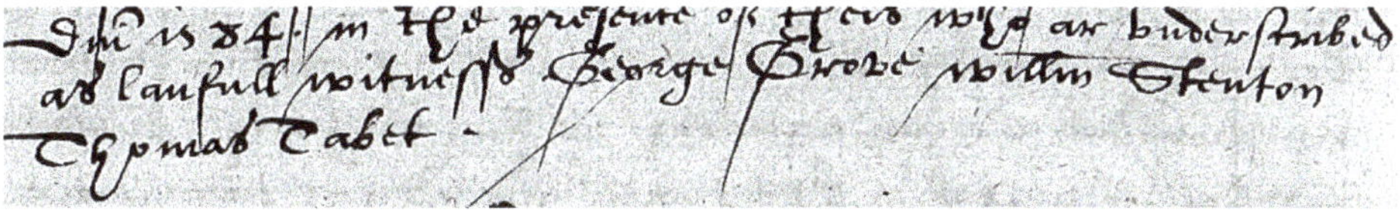

Note:
Line 14 the fourth word appears to be 'shalbe be' with the word 'be' written in error, rather than 'shalle be', compare with the double 'l' in 'lawfull' line 11.

There is limited use of capital letters throughout and generally erratic spelling including the frequently missing final 'e' in words such as 'mak' and 'grac'.

The symbol # has been used to represent a seemingly meaningless pen mark on line 17.

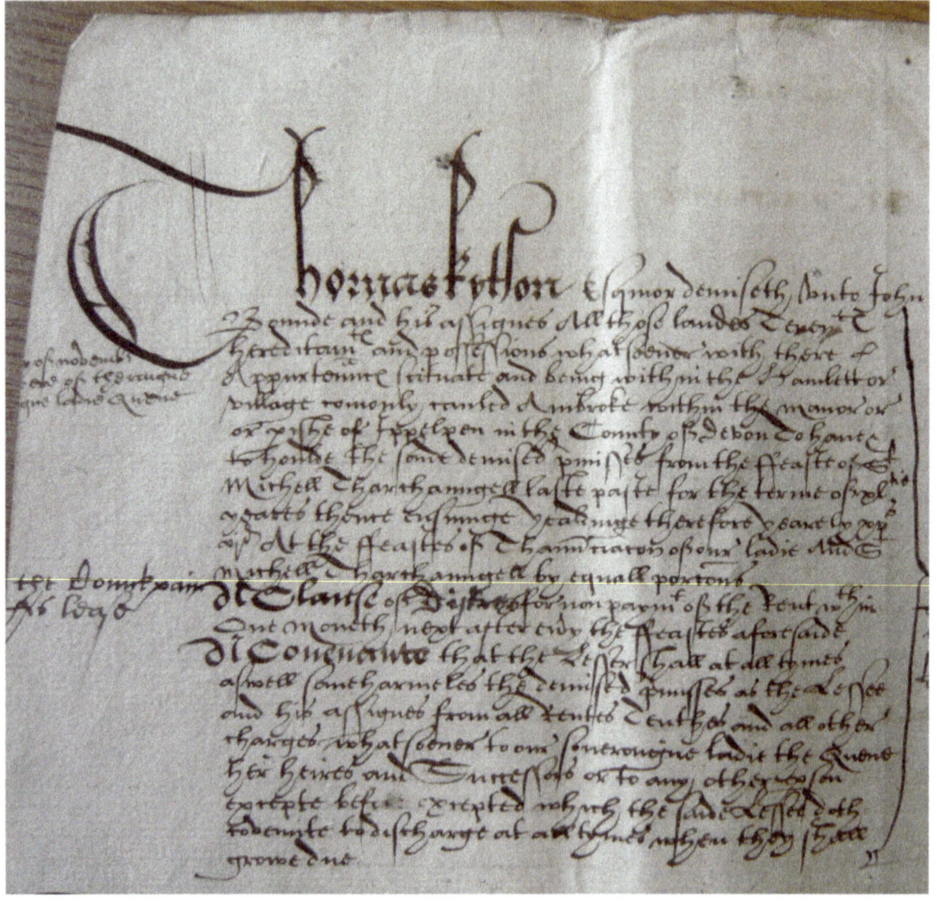

Thomas Fytton Esquior demiseth unto John Bennet and his assignes All those landes tenementes heredytamentes and possessions whatsoever with there appurtenaunce situate and being within the Hamlett or village comonly called Ambroke within the manor or parishe of Hetley in the County of Devon To have to holde the same demised premisses from the ffeaste of St Michell tharchaungell laste paste for the terme of xxi yeares thence ensuinge yealdinge therefore yearely xxs at the ffeastes of Thanunciacon of our ladie and St Michell tharchaungell by equall portions
A clause of Distres for non payment of the rent within one moneth next after eny the ffeastes aforesaide
A Covenaunte that the Lessor shall at all tymes aswell save harmles the demised premisses as the Lessee and his assignes from all rentes tenthes and all other charges whatsoever to our sovereigne ladie the Quene her heires and successors or to any other person excepte before excepted which the saide Lessee doth covenaunte to discharge at all tymes when they shall growe due.

Steward's papers relating to the Devon lands of Sir Thomas Kitson of Hengrave, Suffolk, 1580

Thomas Kytson Esquior demiseth unto John
Bounde and his assignes All those landes Tenem[en]^{tes}
hereditam[en]^{tes} and possessions whatsoever with there #
Appurtenanc[es] scituate and being with in the Hamlett or
village comonly cauled Ambroke within the manor or
or p[ar]ishe of Ippelpen in the County of Devon To have &
to houlde the saide demised p[re]misses from the Feast of St
Michell Tharchanngell laste paste for the terme of xl^{tie}
yeares thence ensuinge yealdinge therefore yearely xv^{s}
vj^{d} At the Feastes of Thanu[n]ciacion of our ladie And St
michell Tharchanngell by equall porc[i]ons
A Clause of Distres for non paym[en]^{t} of the Rent w[i]thin
one moneth next after ev[er]y the Feastes aforesaid
A covenante that the Lesser shall at all tymes
aswell save harmles the demissed p[re]misses as the Lessee
and his assignes from all Rentes Tenthes and all other
charges what soever to our soveraigne ladie the Quene
her heires and Successors or to any other p[er]son
except before excepted which the said Lessee doth
covennte to discharge at all tymes when they shall
growe due

Marginal entries:
Left 1: *...y of november ... yere of the raigne ... gne ladie Quene.* Part of this annotation has been lost when the page was cut from a volume. This entry provided the date when the lease was made.
Left 2: ... *the Count[er]pair ... his lease.* Again part of this annotation is missing. The small curl upwards from the cross of the 't' indicates an 'er' abbreviation.

This is a typical Secretary hand containing some awkward elements.

The abbreviation stroke for 'pre' in *premisses* (lines 7 and 15) is a backwards slash above the 'p'. It is not connected to the letter and overlays the descenders of letters from the line above. It is quite different to the 'er' abbreviation in *every* (line 13). The abbreviations for 'par' in parish (line 6) and 'per' in persons (line 18) are more standard forms, but are confused with letters on the lines below.

Scribes commonly run the definite article into words beginning with a vowel: *Tharchanngell* (the Archangel) and *Thanunciacion* (the Annunciation).

The *Tenthes* (line 16) refers to the collection of a form of national taxation called the Fifteenth and Tenth which was raised on all communities at irregular intervals between 1332 and 1624.

A Survey made of the Mannour there the vth of August Anno [illegible] and in the second and third yeres of the reignes of Phillipp and Mary by the grace of god kyng and quene of England Spayne ffraunce both Cycylles Jerusalem and Ireland Deffendours of the faith Archedukes of Austria Dukes of Burgundy Millayne and Brabant Countes of Haspurge fflaunders and Tyrole for Sir Gyles Strangwaies knight Overseer of the said mannor in Right of mastres Margaret Hennage widowe mother to the said Sir Gyles and nowe the [illegible] of the same mannour by thassent of the said mastres Hennage as hereafter followeth that is to witte

The Customary tenauntes in Compton

Thomas [illegible] holdeth by copy dated xxiiij Octobris Annis regnorum Philippi et Mariae Regis et Reginae [illegible] of the graunte of John [illegible] then Steward [illegible] for a dwellinghouse cont v couples A garden orchard and backsyde cont di acre pasture One close of pasture above meade [illegible] One close of meadowe lying beneth meade cont ij acre One close of meadowe called the myddleclose cont one acre One close of arable lande beside the [illegible] cont ij acre And of arable lande at large in the westfild [illegible] acres [illegible] in theastfeld [illegible] acre with common appendant [illegible] in Hedgmoore To have to hym for terme of his lief onely by the yerely Rent of [illegible] shall heryott his best beaste The fine [illegible]	Rentes [illegible]

A survey of the manor of Compton Dundon, Somerset, 1558

A Survey made of the Mannour there the vth
of August Anno [Latin meaning: *year*] [illegible word] and yn the vth and vjth yeres of
the reignes of
Phillipp and Mary by the grace of god Kyng and quene of Englond
Spaign Fraunce, both Scycyll[es], Jher[usale]m and Irelond, Defendours of
the faith Archydukes of Austria, Dukes of Bourgony, Millaine,
and Braband, Countees of Hamspourgh, Flaundres and Tyroll, for
S[i]^{r} Gyles Strangwaies knyght enherytor of the said Mannour yn Rev[er]c[i]on
of Masteres Margaret Henneage weadowe, mother to the said S[i]^{r} Gyles
and nowe the moynteresse of the same Mannour by thassent of the
said masteres Henneage as hereafter foloweth that is to wete.

The Customary ten[au]nttes yn Compton

Thomas Poulet thoungar holdeth by copy — Renttes
dated xiiij^{o} Octobr Annis regnorum Phi[llippis] et Marie — xxv^{s}
Regne et Regine nunc ij^{o} et ij^{o} of the grauntte of John
Elcockes then S^{ur}veyour One Ten[emen]t builded for a
dwelling howsse con[taining] viij couples. A garden, orchard
and backside con[taining] di[midia] [Latin meaning: *half*] akre pasture.
One close of
pasture above meade cum [Latin meaning: *with*] j akr & di[midia] One close of
meadow lyeing benethe meade cont[aining] ij akr. One close
of meadowe called the Myddleclose con[taining] one akre One
close of arable londe besydes the culverhousse cont[aining]
vj akr and of ar[able] londe at large in the westfild
vj akres et di[midia] & in theastefild xj akr & half
w[i]th common append[a]unt ther and app[ur]ten[au]nt yn
Sedgemoore. To have to hym for terme of his
lief only, by yerly Rent of xxv s[hillings] &
shall heryott his best beaste. The fyne C s[hillings] #

This is one of the earliest and most difficult Secretary hands in this volume. It is notable for containing almost all of the contractions and ligatures discussed in the introduction as well as occasional Latin words, complex dating, Roman numerals and some very peculiar spellings!

The date, in Latin, may be translated: '14th of October in the years of the reigns of Phillipp and Mary King and Queen now the 2nd and 2nd'.

Note that there are abbreviation strokes over some words in which no letters have been omitted, for instance 'John' (line 14) and 'common' (line 24).

A medieval court hand has been used for the introductory line, the first words of the sub-heading and the second paragraph. The use of a different writing style was a common method of highlighting headings.

The definite article is sometimes run into the following word particularly when it begins with a vowel: 'thoungar' for 'the younger' (line 12) and 'theastefild' for 'the east field' (line 23).

Decanatus de Albury

Albury — D Robertus Stokynges vic

Andrewe mortymer — They presente that they have
Bryan Clyve — no carpett to lay uppon the
Johannes Shotes — comunion table in defaulte
Richard Spenser — of the parishens. Item they presente

that Robert Cocke and Edithe
Haborley fornicate but the forsaid
John Shotes have lyved ~~incontinently~~ in avoutrye
to the evill example of others Item Richard payne
hathe lyved ~~in~~ in avoutrye with Anne Clyfford
and Anne mortymer Item that Anne ~~Clyve~~ Webbe
Sengle woman hath borne a childe in the parishe that she
lyved w[ith] in [illegible] Item they presente that they have
not theire quarterly sermons accordinge to the kinges
injunctions

Aston Ro[illegible] — D Rob[illegible] Kente cur

John Hall — They presente that the Chauncell
John Jones — wyndowes lyeth open and that the
Edwarde Rawlyns — Chauncell ys not made playne

that the table lacketh a frame
a carpett or a clothe [illegible] and
there lacketh clene clothes for the [illegible] and
also there lacketh the paraphrases for the [illegible]
of Erasmus

Bishop's visitation, deanery of Avebury, Avebury and Alton Priors, Wiltshire, 1553

Decanatus de Avebury [Latin meaning: *Deanery of Avebury*]

Avebury

D[ominus] [Latin meaning; *father, lord or master depending upon the context*] Robertus Stvynson vic[arius] [Latin meaning: *vicar*]

Andreas mortymer	} They p[re]sente that they have
Ric[ard]us Olyv[er] }ico[nomi]	} no carpett to lay uppon the
Joh[an]nes Schoter } [Latin meaning:	} co[mm]union Table in defaulte
Ric[ar]dus Spencer }*churchwardens*]	} of the p[ar]ysshen[er]s It[em] they p[re]sente
	} that Robert Cokk[es] and Edith
	} haberby s[e]rva[u]nte unto the forsaid

John Shoter have lyvid ~~incontine[n]tly~~ in incontin[en]cye
to the Evill Example of others It[e]m Richard Payne
hathe lyvid ~~inc~~ in incontin[en]cye with Amye clyfford
and Jone Mortymer It[e]m that Jone ~~Ryve~~ Reve
Senglewoma[n] that bo[ur]ne a childe & the p[ar]tye that she
used w[i]th is fladd It[em] they p[re]sent that they have
not theyre qarters s[e]rmans according to the ki[n]ges ma[jes]tes Iniu[n]ctions

Alto[n] p[ri]ors

D[ominus] Ric[ardu]s		Kent Cur[atus] [Latin meaning: *curate*]
Joh[an]es Hudd	} ico[nomi]	} they p[re]sente that the chauncell
Joh[an]es Maurez	} [*churchwardens*)]	} wyndows lyeth open and that the
Edwarde Rawlyn	}	} chau[n]cell ys not made playne &
		a carpett or a cloth upon hyt and
		ther lackyth clene clothes for the co[muni]o[n]
		also ther lackyth the parafres[u]s of erasmus.

An extremely cursive and difficult hand in which the suspension marks for 'm', 'n' and 'u' appear within, not above, the word. There are many instances of letters being so poorly formed that they appear as a horizontal line.

Note: the open topped small 'a', and the capitals 'H' and 'P', which are simply enlarged versions of the small letters.

The Injunctions of Edward VI (line 16) required the parish priest to preach in person four times each year in the parish church. The chancel was to be made plain (line 20) to remove Catholic imagery. *The Paraphrases of the Bible* by Erasmus (line 24) was required reading in the post Reformation church.

Item paid for ~~candles for~~ xxiiii^ti pounds of candles for the same weyke viii pounds &
iiii d — vi s viii d Item paid to Richard Elyott for v pounds of wax made in
together for the church — ii s viii d

Item paid for a fyre panne for the churche — x d Item paid for making of the barrs
of the west dore — vi d Item for nayles for the scaffold — ii d Item for making of
a gemowe for ~~the~~ [illegible] — ii d Item for making of ~~a bottom~~ of the sensor — iiii d
Item paid for a ~~bell~~ bokell for the v th bell — ii d Item for a key for the tower
dore — ii d Item for making of a key & for mending of the lock of the [illegible]
dore of the ambulatory — iiii d Item paid for mending of the lock of the almeshouse
dore — ii d Item paid for oyle for the bells — iiii d

Item paid to Walter Vyncent for keping of the bells all the yere — xx d Item paid to Walter
Vyncent for mending of the baldryke for the bells — iiii d Item paid to a carpenter for
mending of the iiii bell whells — iiii d Item for nayles for the same whells — ii d

Item paid to Thomas Osmondes man for taking of the grett bell clapp to Ilmester to
making and for bryngyng ~~the~~ to Ilmester agayne & fetche yt — ii s Item paid to
John Cuttelor for making of the pastall taper — ii s viii d

Item paid to John Cuttelor for making of [illegible] — ii s ii d Item paid to the same John
for mending of the vestymentts — xii d Item for v yerdes of sylke to sowe the said
vestymentts with — ii s Item for ii skaynes of sylke for the same vestymentts iiii d

Item paid to Thomas plomer for a C of ledde for the churche laid upon the west ende
of the walke of the said churche — iii s vi d Item paid to Roger Smyth for
mending of the claper of the v th bell — iii s iiii d

Item paid for frankensence — iiii d Item paid for wasshyng of ye churche clothes
— ii s iiii d Item for paper for this boke of accompte — ii d Item paid for keping of
this boke all the hole yere and for making of the same boke at this
accompte — vi s

Sherborne, Dorset, Churchwardens' Accounts, 1543

It[e]m paid for ~~sowder fo~~ xxiij^{li} pounde of sowder for the same warke ev[er]y pounde
iiij^{d} – vij^{s} viij^{d} It[e]m paid to Richard Elyott for v pounde of wax made in
torches for the churche – ij^{s} vj^{d}

It[e]m paid for a fyer panne for the churche – x^{d} It[e]m paid for makyng of the barre
of the West dore – vj^{d} It[e]m for nayles for the scafold – ij^{d} It[e]m for makyng of
a gemowe for the treangle ij^{d} It[e]m for makyng of a bottom for the sensor iiij^{d}

It[e]m paid for a ~~bell~~ bokell for the vth bell – j^{d} It[em] for a key for the tower
dore - ij^{d} It[em] for makyng of a kay & for mendyng of the loke of the Sowthe
dore of the ambulatory – iiij^{d} It[e]m paid for mendyng of the loke of the Almeshowse
dore – ij^{d} It[e]m paid for oyle for the bell[es] – iiij^{d}

It[e]m paid to Walter Vyncent for kepyng of the bell[es] all the yere – xx^{d} It[e]m paid to Walte^{r}
Vyncent for mendyng of the bawdryk[es] for the bell[es] - iiij^{d} It[e]m paid to a Carpent[e]^{r} for #
mendyng of the iiijth bell whelle – iiij^{d} It[e]m for nayles for the same whelle – ij^{d}

It[e]m paid to Thomas Osmond[es] man for caryng of the grett bell clep[er] to Ilmest[e]^{r} to
makyng and for Rydyng ~~thef~~ to Ilmest[e]^{r} a gayne to fatche yt - ij^{s} It[e]m paid to
John Butteler for makyng of the pascall taper – ij^{s} viij^{d}

It[e]m paid to John Butteler for makyng of Torches – iij^{s} ij^{d} It[e]m paid to the same John
for mendyng of the Vestymentt[es] - xij^{d} It[e]m for vj yard[es] of Sylke to hem[m]e the said
Vestymentt[es] w[i]^{t}[h]all - ij^{s} It[e]m for ij Skaynes of Sylke for the same Vestymentt[es] iiij^{d}

It[e]m paid to Thomas plomer for a C of ledde for the churche laid uppon the West ende
of the bulke of the said Churche – iiij^{s} viij^{d} It[e]m paid to Roger Smyth for
mendyng of the cleper of the vth bell – iij^{s} iiij^{d}

It[e]m paid for frankencence – iiij^{d} It[e]m paid for Wasshyng of þe churche clothes
- iij^{s} iiij^{d} It[e]m for paper for this boke of accompte – ij^{d} It[e]m for kepyng of
this boke all the hole yere and for makyng of the same boke at this
accompte v^{s}

A very clear mid-sixteenth century hand containing some difficult features and characteristically medieval letter forms, notably 'w', often indistiguishable between small letters and capitals.

Note: the mark at the end of line 15 to fill the line, represented in the transcript by the symbol '#'.

The capital 'C' for a hundred, line 26.

This scribe usually uses 'th' when writing 'the' but once uses the character thorn, line 30, here represented as 'þ' for distinction, but usually transcribed as 'th'.

'A gemowe for the treangle' probably means a hinge for the triptych (an altarpiece with three panels), or a hinge for a triangular structure for storing vestments.

Ryght worshypfull Syr In my moste hertyest maner I recomend me unto
yow certyffyeng yow that I have resseyved yor gentle lettr wher by I perceve
that ye suppose thyse ther shulde be certeyne releffes behynde dew unto yow
for my maner of Holford Syr trew hyt ys that ther ys one releffe be
hynde dew unto yow for my seyd maner upon the deth of my father / for I
knowe well that I holde the seyd maner of yow as of yowr maner of
Compton Dundon by knyghts servyce but by what quantyte of tenure I
can not tell wher for I am uncerteyne how mych the releff shulde be
but for as moche as I knowe yor worshyp to be suche and yor good wyll
also to me that ye wyll demaunde but yor dew / I do ther for remytte hyt
unto yor self how mych hyt shulde be wher of yf hyt be yor pleysure to
certefye me by thys berer / I shall send yow money incontynent. And
that pleysure that lyeth yn my symple power ys / shall be at yowr
comandement as knowyth Jhesu who ever have yow yn hys blessed
kepyng wryten at Comtonhawey the xxvjti day of October by

yowrs at comandement
Thomas Stradlyng

Letter from Thomas Stradling to Sir Giles Strangways relating to the manor of Halsway, Somerset, *circa* 1540

Ryght worshypfull Syr In my moste hertyest maner I Reco[m]mend me unto
yow certyffyeng yow that I have Rescevyd yo[ur] gentle lett[er] wher by I perceve
that ye suppose ~~that~~ ther sholde be certeyne Relyefes behynde dew unto yow
for my maner of Halswey / Syr trew hyt ys that ther ys one Relyeffe be
hynde dew unto yow for my seyd maner upon the deth of my father / for I
knowe well that I holde the seyd maner of yow as of yowr maner of
Compton Dundene by knyȝhts s[er]vyce / but by whate quantyte of tenure I
can not tell / wher for I am uncerteyne how moche the Releif sholde be
but for as moche as I knowe yo[u]^{r} worshyp to be suche / and yo[u]^{r} good wyll
also to me that ye wyll demaunde but yo[u]^{r} dew / I do ther for remytte hyt
unto yo[u]^{r} self how moche hyt sholde be wher of yf hyt be y[ou]^{r} pleysure to
asserteyne me by thys berer / I shall send you money incontynent. And
that pleysure that lyeth yn my Symple power ys & shall be at yowr
com[m]aundeme[n]t as knowyth Ihu (*a contraction of Ihesu, i.e. Jesus*) who ev[er] have yow
yn hys blessyd
kepyng wryten at Comton Hawey the xxvj^{ti} day of October by
Y[our]s at com[m]aundement
Thomas Stradlyng

A clear and well spaced mid sixteenth century hand owing much to its medieval antecedents.

Note: the use of the faint forward slashes for punctuation and the character yogh in *knyȝhts*, line 7, quite different from the 'g' in *Ryght*, line 1. However, the word 'ye' (line 3) is the second person singular pronoun, usually modern 'you', and the character thorn is not used by this scribe.

The long 's' resembles an 'f', so Halswey, line 4, could easily be mis-read as Halfwey.

The spelling is difficult at times, but the meaning usually becomes clear when the words are read aloud, in cases where words such as behind (lines 4 through to 5) have been divided in two.

xxiiij^to die January A^o xx^o H viij^ui

fforasmoche as John Dorset executo^r of the testament of John Nelle otherwise called John Barforde late of the pyshe of Mellet in the Countie of Somset decessed psonally apered afor the kyngs honorable Counsell the day and yere afore reherset. And then and there openly confessed that the contents of the bill of complaint by hym presented vnto the kyngs grace wherupon he obteigned his graciouse tres directed to certain Comyssions named vpon the same for the heryng and examynacon of the trouthe and playnnes therin conteigned against thabbot of Glastonbury ye were falsly fayned and vntrue. as the same John Dorset aswell afore the said Counsaill as the said Comyssions affirmed, yet neuertheles the same Abbot of his charitie and good mynde frely forgave and remytted the same John all suche losse cost and damage as he by force of the same hath susteigned and borne in the onely defence of the said cause notwithstanding the vntrue demaund^s afore specified. Wherupon the said Counsaill have dismyssed and dyscharged the same Abbot and his Counsaill lerned of any further sute therin to bee made afore them at the desyre of the said John Dorset. commaundyng hym ~~further~~ that he in noowise heraft^r make any like vntrue surmyse against the said Abbot ne any other pson. vpon payne of Imprysonement ~

Court of requests, appearances, final orders and decrees, Hillary Term 14 Henry VIII, 1524

xxiiij^to die Januarij Anno &c[etera] ~~xxiiij~~^o

Forasmoche as John Dorset executo[ur] of the testement of John Newe
otherwise called John Barforde late of the p[ar]yshe of Melles in the
Countie of Som[er]set decessed p[er]sonnally apered afor the King[es] hono[ur]able
Counsaill the day and yere afor rehersed and then and ther
openly confessed that the content[es] of the bill of complaint by hym
presented unto the King[es] grace wherupon he obleigued his gracious
bre[vis] [Latin meaning: writ] directed to certain Comyssion[er]s named upon the same for the
hering and examynacou[n] of the trouthe and playnnes therin
conteigned against thabbot of Glastonbury / ys clierly fayned
and untrue as the same John Dorset aswell affor the said
Counsaill as the said Comyssion[er]s affyrmed / yet nev[er]theles
the same Abbot of his charitie and good mynde frely forgave
and remytted the same John all suche losse cost[es] and damag[es]
as he by force of the same hathe susteigned and borne in the
oonly defence of the said cause notw[i]^t[h]standing the untrue demeano[ur]
afor specified / Wherupon the said Counsaill have dismyssed
and dyscharged the same Abbot and his Counsaill Lerned
of any further sute therin to bee made afor therin at the
desyre of the said John Dorset com[m]anding hym ~~by the~~
that he in nowise heraft[er] make any lyke untrue surmyse
against the said Abbot ne any other p[er]son upon payne of
Imprysonement

A clear early sixteenth century hand in which the inflience of medieval forms is still very evident.

Note: the scribe uses two different forms of capital 'C' in Countie and Counsaill.

The date, in Latin, may be translated as: '24th January in the 14th year etc.' From the context of this volume this is clearly the 14th year of the reign of Henry VIII, 1524]

The scribe uses a forward slash as punctuation to indicate the end of a paragraph or the start of a new section.

Abbreviations are particularly difficult when words are run together as in notw[i]^t[h] standing (line 15).

Note; two forms of terminal 's' in 'Melles' (line 3) and 'Comyssioners' (line 8) as well as a terminal 'es' contraction in 'Kinges' (line 4) and long 's' in the middle of words like 'Dorset' (line 2).

Letter from the abbot of Cerne Abbey, 1510–1524

Ryghte Wurschipfull in my moste hartyest man[er] I Recom[m]end me unto
you And the cawse of my W[ri]tynge unto you ys for the money thatt
I have d[elivere]^{d} to the p[ri]st for you for thys yere past for h[i]^{s} s[er]vyce the whyche
Syngyth for my Lady Carew god p[ar]don her Sowle the s[u]m ys vj li xiij^{s}
iiij^{d} I wule ^{nott} send you att thys ~~ty~~ tyme butt for very nede now
A geynst thys goode season moreov[er] there ys A nodyr Rekenyng by twyxte
you & me the whyche yf h[i]^{t} may please you to Reme[m]bre And att yo^{ur} leys[er]
of the whyche Rekenyngs my S[er]vaund thys berer d[elivere]^{d} you a byll of att
Stynsford h[i]^{t} may please you all so to send me the same S[u]m of the
seyd Rekenyngs ye schall bynd me by the same hereaft[er] to do any thyngs
thatt ys in me ^{to} do As oure lord knowyth who p[re]s[er]ve you Scryblyd
in hast the iiijth day of thys p[re]sant monyth of Ap[ri]ll w[i]^{t} the hand of
all yo[urs] to my power

Robert Abbott of Cerne

This is a difficult hand incorporating features of both Secretary and medieval hands.

The abbreviation for 'ser' appears in 'servyce' (line 3), 'Leyser' (i.e. 'leisure', line 7) and the more difficult 'servaund' (i.e. 'servant', line 8).

The three 'p' abbreviations are found in 'prist' (line 3), 'pardon' (line 4) and 'presant' (line 12).

The meaning of abbreviations such as 'd^{d}' for 'delivered' (lines 3 and 8) may only be established by the context and by reading the text aloud, which also makes it is easier to recognise the meaning of 'hit', for 'it', or 'A nodyr' for 'another'.

Note that 'h' has completely lost its shoulder ('the' and 'thatt' line 2) and the high lead stroke coming into 'w' in 'Carew' and 'Sowle' (line 4) which does not appear in 'cawse' (line 2).

Letter from Hugh Parker to his father James Parker, Lancashire, *circa* 1490

Ryrght trusty and welbelovyd fad[u]^{r} & modyr I com[m]awnd me unto you sekyng you of yo^{ur} blessyyng[es] &c Fadur I pray you send me
word w^{h}edyr ʒe have laburd to my lord strange for me Þ[a]^{t} I may goo w[i]t hym[m] or not, yff so be Þ[a]^{t} I shall not goo w[i]^{t} hym[m] I p[ra]y you
send me word has schortly has ʒe kanne for I shall goo w[i]t a nod[er]. Also I pray you that ʒe wyll speke for thomas my kinnis
man[n]e for ʒe wyll $^{cum[m]e}$ w[i]^{t} me. I pray you send me word whedyr ʒe ~~ye~~ goo yo[u]r selfe or not / No mor[e] but ih[es]u kepe you wrytyn
at ov'hampton In Vigilea An[*unciat*]is b[eat]e marie &c.
By your son[n]e }
Hew Parker }

This is an early example of private correspondence from the north of England, though it was written not by the sender but by a clerk or secretary. It is notable for the use of a fine, regular hand, indicating a trained and literate person (Hugh Parker's own hand is much less sophisticated and elegant). More important though is that this document employs both of the obsolete Anglo-Saxon letters still in use at this time: yogh (ʒ) appears instead of 'y' at the beginning of the word 'ye' (i.e. 'thee'), which is the plural of the word 'you' and here is probably intended to convey that <u>both</u> parents are being addressed [since the word 'you' is also employed]. The letter thorn (Þ), signifying 'th', is found twice, in the word Þ[a]t, meaning 'that'. In this example, so that the original spelling is emphasised, the transcription does not modernise the two letters, although this would be normal practice.

Note: the double 'y' in blessyyng[es] (line 1). One of the problems with transcription is instinctive correction of spelling and making assumptions based upon modern spellings. When making a literal transcription it is always necessary to re-check transcripts for these accidental corrections.

The place *ov'hampton* is almost certainly Wolverhampton and the transcription should therefore read ov[er]hampton, but an apostrophe has been left in the transcript to indicate one of the ways in which ambiguities may be notated.

The original text is damaged on the final line at the word 'An[*unciat*]is' but the meaning is clear and so has been inserted in italics in square brackets; the eve (*Vigilia*) of the Feast of the Annunciation of Our Lady is the 24 March, but as no year is given the document cannot be securely dated.

Documents used in this volume

Chiswick, Middlesex, the household expenses of Sir Stephen Fox, 1680, Dorset History Centre, D-FSI/Box211.

East Harnham, Wiltshire, petition of the inhabitants to the Quarter Sessions, Hilary term 1673, Wiltshire and Swindon History Centre, A110/1673H/110.

Newport, Monmouthshire, three exemption certificates for the Hearth Tax, 1664, the National Archives, E179/335.

Scopwick, Lincolnshire, Hearth Tax assessment, 1664, the National Archives, E179/335.

Broadwey, Upwey and Nottington, Dorset, final concord (or final agreement), 1653, Dorset History Centre, D-GOO/2922.

Alchester, Oxfordshire, love letter from Fulk Madeley, 1652, Surrey History Centre, LM/COR/6/4.

Maldon, Essex, customs book, 1649, the National Archives, E122/226/56.

Dorchester, Dorset, calendar of the House of Correction, 1629, Dorset History Centre, Q/S/M/1/1.

Thornhill, Gummershay, Caundle Wake and Stourton Caundle, Dorset, lay subsidy, 1628, Dorset History Centre, D-FSI, acc.10498.

Dalham, Suffolk, glebe terrier, 1613, Suffolk Record Office, Bury St Edmunds, E14/4/1.

Calne, Wiltshire, presentment of the constables of Calne borough to the Quarter Sessions, 1612, Wiltshire and Swindon History Centre, A110/1612E/177.

Salisbury, Wiltshire, letter of Juell Longe to the official of the bishop of Salisbury, undated, probably 1612, Wiltshire and Swindon History Centre, D1/35/1/3.

Brightwell Baldwin, Oxfordshire, parish register, 1598-1605, Oxfordshire History Centre, PAR40/1/R1/1.

Gillingham, Dorset, licence for a parishioner to eat meat during Lent, 1595, Dorset History Centre, PE-GIL/RE/1/1.

Hengrave Park, Suffolk, account book, 1587, Suffolk Record Office, Bury St Edmunds, HA/528/5730/113.

Kettering, Northamptonshire, survey by Ralph Treswell, 1585, Northamptonshire Record Office, LM/272.

Henley, Oxfordshire, will of Bastian Bond, 1584, Oxfordshire History Centre.

Ipplepen, Devon, steward's papers relating to the Devon lands of Sir Thomas Kitson, 1580, Suffolk Record Office, Bury St Edmunds, HA E3/15/53/1/1.

Compton Dundon, Somerset, survey of the manor, 1558, Dorset History Centre, D-FSI/Box24.

Avebury and Alton Priors, Wiltshire, Bishop's visitation of the deanery of Avebury, 1553, Wiltshire and Swindon History Centre, D1/43/1.

Sherborne, Dorset, churchwardens' accounts, 1543, Dorset History Centre, PE-SH/CW/1/20.

Halsway, Somerset, letter from Thomas Stradling to Sir Giles Strangways, *circa* 1540, Dorset History Centre, D-FSI/Box233(doc1).

Mells, Somerset, dispute in the Court of Requests, 1524, the National Archives, REQ/1/5.

Cerne Abbas, Dorset, letter from the Abbot of Cerne Abbey, 1510-1524, Dorset History Centre, D-FSI/Box233(doc2).

Lancashire, letter from Hugh Parker to his father James Parker, *circa* 1490, Lancashire Archives, DDHK 9/1/9.

www.ingramcontent.com/pod-product-compliance
Ingram Content Group UK Ltd.
Pitfield, Milton Keynes, MK11 3LW, UK
UKHW062304290726
14090UKWH00017B/874